Endorsen

In a world where there are far too many barriers and never enough bridges, Pam Morton's words span daunting cultural chasms with compassion, understanding, humor, and hope. Through her book, *One Plane Ticket From Normal*, a thoroughly engaging read, I laughed, cried, and pondered my way to a new perspective of what it's like to totally uproot from *normal* life and move to an "other" culture where *you* are actually the "other." I appreciated Morton's candid glimpse into the delights and difficulties of learning a new language, deciphering unfamiliar customs, and connecting with those who we in the West often view with suspicion. Her short bursts of wisdom at the end of each chapter in a section called *Culture Cue* offer invaluable insights for those who travel internationally (I'm taking notes) or for anyone who wants to befriend "other culture" folks in their own community (yep, I'm taking notes again).

There is much to love about this informative, yet heartwarming book. But what I love most about *One Plane Ticket From Normal* is the poignant reminder that people are people are people, the world over. And those *other culture* people, so precious to God, can become precious to us...especially if we are willing to take a step or two away from "normal." After reading this book, I'm in.

Dr. Jodi Detrick
Author of *The Jesus-Hearted Woman*
Former *Seattle Times* Columnist
Certified Leadership Coach

One Plane Ticket From Normal is an incredible read! Pam's humor and gifted story-telling will keep you turning the pages and wishing the book was longer. She shares such great insights for engaging people from other cultures, that you will find yourself longing for experiences of your own. Her love for the people of the Middle East stirs something deep in my heart—a desire to love big and sacrificially.

Kerry Clarensau
Speaker, Mentor, Author, Leader of women
Author of *Fully His Devotional, Selah Devotional, A Beautiful Life: Discovering the Freedom of Selfless Love, Redeemed! Embracing a Transformed Life, Love Revealed, The Love Revealed Challenge,* and *Secrets: Transforming Your Life and Marriage.*

This book is a passport to a totally different perspective on what it means to follow Christ. With warmth and humor, Pam shares her family's transition from middle America to life in the Middle East. *One Plane Ticket From Normal* will make you laugh and inspire you to take a faith journey of your own.

John & Debbie Lindell
Lead Pastors, James River Church, Ozark, MO
Author of *She Believes*

One Plane Ticket From Normal

Foreword by Kary Oberbrunner

Pamela J. Morton

ONE PLANE
TICKET
FROM
NORMAL

Your Humorous and Hope-Filled
Guide to Life in the Middle East

One Plane Ticket From Normal

Pamela J. Morton

ISBN: 978-1-943526-27-7
Library of Congress Control Number: 2016914372
Author Academy Elite

Author Academy Elite, Powell, OH
Printed in the United States of America

Cover design: Nl_studio Tbilisi, Georgia
Interior design: JETLAUNCH.net

Dedication

To my family, John, Emileigh, Aria
You lived this adventure with me and loved through it all.

To my friends in the Middle East
You welcomed us with open arms. We are forever changed.

To Jesus
Thank you for calling me beyond what's comfortable to a life
that's full of stretching, hope and richness.

Contents

Foreword

I don't laugh out loud many times, especially when reading a book. But as I dove into *One Plane Ticket From Normal*, I couldn't help myself.

Although I don't have plans to visit the Middle East in the near future, while reading Pam's book I found myself transported to a world I've only seen in pictures.

Besides entertainment, Pam's book delivered a shot of serious value in a number of areas:

I found her snapshots of daily life for those who want to know what it's like to live in another part of the world—eye-opening.

I found her stories of friends made along the way that reveal Middle Eastern thought and lifestyle—helpful.

I found her culture cues, tips for integrating into new cultures, interacting with other-culture persons and creating safe environments for deep-life conversations—relevant.

And I found her discussion questions for small group studies—practical.

In today's digitally connected world, we are now global citizens. We can't afford to isolate. If we do, we sign up for irrelevance and self-sabotage our message. *One Plane Ticket From Normal* shows you the way to increase your global IQ in an educationally entertaining way.

Brace yourself for impact—literally. Pam—your tour guide—is a creative and energetic communicator who gives insight for interacting with other-culture people in a meaningful, fun, approachable way.

Read her words and you'll be entertained. Practice her words and you'll be enlightened.

Kary Oberbrunner
CEO of Redeem the Day and Igniting Souls
Co-creator of Author Academy Elite
Author of *Elixir Project, Day Job to Dream Job, The Deeper Path,* and *Your Secret Name.*

Preface

The stories you are about to read are true. I was there. The names of our friends, however, have been changed for privacy. These dear people have opened their lives and hearts to us. I, in gratitude, will protect their identities.

Not every interaction we have had made it into the book. First, there are too many stories to tell; second, I want to pull back the curtain on individual people's lives rather than the sensational that consumes so many news headlines about this part of the world.

I am not naive as to what is happening in the Middle East or sugar-coating it. Society struggles; travesties occur. I have lived it. Daily we ask God to give us wisdom and compassionate hearts.

We have contingency plans, political "snow days" and embassy hotline numbers. However, I have chosen to balance the scales a bit by describing the positive interactions we have experienced which far outweigh the negative ones.

Walk with me as we search for an apartment with Hamdee, share water with Miriam and drink tea with Zaheen. Your heart will be altered. Are you ready?

Now that the air is clear, *yallabena*! (Let's go!)

Pam

Introduction

My host smiled, stretched out his hand and offered me a perfectly round goat eyeball. The blue iris glistened under the lone bulb illuminating the interior of this bare-walled concrete home. I am mesmerized. It seemed to actually wink at me. I wait for our host to burst into laughter dispelling the building tension. None came. I am the guest and therefore receive the "best" part of the evening dinner.

My mind wanders to a meal I had had in the States a few months before. Surrounded by friends I laughed at their jokes, recognized the food (none of which stared back) and understood all of it. It felt *normal*. It *was* my normal.

A grunt brought me back to my senses as the gleeful protagonist moved the eyeball closer. I realize in that moment that a 30-hour flight had brought me here to this strange place filled with bizarre customs and, in my opinion, highly questionable food choices. How could one plane ride from Missouri make me feel as though I had landed on Mars?

Absolutely everything is different. Then it hit me, I was simply one plane ticket from normal...back to a place I knew, understood and loved. Dorothy, could point and click (with her computer mouse and a decent credit line) and be back to Kansas...er, Missouri in less time than it would take to grill Billy's brother.

But Jesus was asking me, "Pam, do you want a normal, predictable life or a comfort-stretching, edge-of-faith one?"

I still look in the mirror and ask myself that question every day.

Could I possibly learn to love and live among the people who call the Middle East their home? Am I willing to let go of "normal" to demonstrate the love of an extraordinary Savior?

The following pages are a collection of stories accumulated from our time in Egypt and Sudan. We have lived in a metropolis (Cairo), a city (Khartoum) and a small village along the Nile in Upper Egypt. We have met some beautiful, dear souls and have lived life beyond anything we could have imagined (including various goat parts).

You will find that other-culture friends are not so very different when it comes to love for family, desire for security and a longing to be known by God. Things that are different are sometimes hilarious, sometimes sobering, but all a reflection of a God who loves displaying creativity in mankind.

Following each story is a Culture Cue to help you interact with other-culture people you may meet in your day-to-day life. They will be grateful you tried to interact. *I'm* the other-culture person in this country and every smile, nod or kindness is truly appreciated.

Discussion questions provide opportunity for intercultural dialogue and examination among friends or a small group.

Get your ticket ready; we'll board together. Life will never be the same.

Part 1
The Metropolis • Cairo, Egypt

1

Pam · Where Am I?

Know Why You're There, Ease the Chaos

My eyes opened slowly as I thought I heard a donkey braying for someone to dial 911. I shook my head trying to wake myself from what I was sure was a bizarre food-induced dream. I could still hear the donkey.

I sat up in my bed and looked around. John lay perfectly still, unmoved by it all. I did not hear Emileigh or Aria stirring. I assumed they, too, were still asleep.

I'll just go down and pour myself a Diet Coke, I thought.

Then I realized the door was in the wrong spot. There were no stairs. I, in fact, was not in my home. I was not even in Missouri. It came rushing back: the tearful goodbyes, the endless packing, the building excitement, the long plane ride. Wait! I know where I am. I'm in Egypt, for crying out loud!

Panic rose to my throat as I began questioning every decision we had made to this point. What have we done? What am I doing here? Did we really sell all our possessions? Could I have possibly agreed to live so far away from family, friends, a Hobby Lobby or Panera?

No amount of talking or pinching could bring me out of the reality I was now standing in. We had stepped across the line. John, our two teenaged daughters and I had knowingly and willfully chosen to

3

leave our deeply loved life in Missouri for a land we had never seen, for people we had yet to meet and a life we did not understand.

No amount of talking or pinching could bring me out of the reality I was now standing in.

I sat down in a rather worn chair and put my head in my hands. "Lord, this is for You and for Your glory. I can't imagine carving out a life in a place so very different from what I know, but I choose to trust you.

"You love the people here.
You know them by name.
They are not strange to You.
Would You help me in this moment?
Would You help me every second of every day from now on?
I am going to need it. I *know* I will.

"I want to serve these beautiful people, but I'm scared, panicked, inadequate. Did I mention that I'm loud-mouthed? Yeah...so, if You think this is a good idea then I'll really try to figure this out, hopefully without becoming a lead story on *NBC News*. Deal? Amen."

Smiling, Aria walked in asking what time it was. I looked at my phone. Exactly 5 minutes had passed since the first bray of the donkey. Wow. One year in Cairo may feel like a very long time. However, life is not lived in chunks but rather in moments. Our moment had come. It was time to begin living our new, strange, unknown, wonderful life now.

Culture Cue

Other-culture people may feel a sense of confusion when they first arrive to a new place. You can show true kindness if you give them a Welcome Basket containing fruit, candy and a card listing the names, addresses and phone numbers of a nearby grocery store, pharmacy, library, church and your information.

2

Mark and Mahmoud · Perfume and Dervishes
Embrace Culture, Leave Your House

The lingering jet lag kept me in a constant Benadryl-like haze, but we knew we needed to get moving to fight off its effects. John created a challenge for us each day to give us reason to explore and grow a little more brave with every accomplishment. Today's challenge: Find the big market, *Khan al Khalili*, that we had read about in all the guidebooks and buy one thing. Sounded easy enough. It is *only* one of the largest cities in the world.

We stood on the curb at the base of our hotel lined up neatly and looking every bit as out-of-place as we felt. John began motioning for a taxi in the continuous stream of honking transport. One swerved straight for us and corrected just in time. He yelled out his window, "Yes? *Tax?*" (They say "tax" not "taxi.") John nodded and showed the man a picture of the market which he had wisely put on his phone. A picture truly is worth a thousand words, especially when you do not know one word of Arabic.

The driver said, "Yes! Yes! I take you!" and began zigzagging through the bumper-to-bumper traffic until he parked right in the middle of the sprawling market. We piled out of the old, rusty Peugeot and were immediately pushed along by local shoppers who knew exactly what they wanted and where they wanted to go. We were wide-eyed and slow to start.

John took off in a direction and motioned for us to follow. Through the tiny little corridors, where hundreds of years of ancient trade had taken place, we were first greeted by a young man named Mark.

"I was born in Ohio. I come to Egypt when I am 2. I speak good English. You come look at my 100-year shop," said Mark.

My husband smiled and told him, "Sure." (John is a really nice guy. I am less nice when nervous and concerned about potential kidnapping scenarios.)

We each were given a seat in a cramped corner of his fully-stocked shop. He addressed Emileigh as Cleopatra, Aria as Nefertiti, John as Ramses and me as Queen of the Nile. He was quite a showman. He began smearing a wide variety of perfumes on us and telling us he "makes us a good deal for perfume which will not spill on plane." He obviously had had many tourists before.

> **It was an unrehearsed dance in chaos.**

He and John bartered back and forth for several minutes. Reaching an impasse, we began our exit to declare our displeasure with his prices. He pulled John back in. Within a few minutes John was the proud owner of three bottles of Egyptian perfume for his "queens."

We continued bobbing and dodging vendors with every possible type of mercantile item. Women balanced baskets on their heads. Men used dollies to carry their burden of goods through uneven streets. Cats scurried between legs. It was an unrehearsed dance in chaos.

Happy to have accomplished our task, we secured a taxi back to the hotel. We rested a bit before John announced he had arranged for a Nile dinner cruise. We prepared to meet our host, Mahmoud.

Mahmoud arrived on time and nicely dressed in Levi jeans, a pink Ralph Lauren polo and trendy Italian glasses. He drove us through the ultra sleek downtown area of Cairo in a compact car which had suffered dings and scrapes from the Indy-driving style of local commuters.

Where do they park the camels? I wondered. Maybe Egypt was more modernized than I thought.

Mahmoud escorted us to a large boat decorated in Christmas lights. He directed us to the dining level where a table was reserved near the band stage.

Soon, several busloads of Asian tourists arrived and filled in the blank spots around us. Our evening began when the band members sang in broken English Stevie Wonder's song, "I just called to say I love you." I was singing along and having a great time. They moved on to Lionel Richie and again I knew all the words. If they had held a karaoke contest, I would have totally dominated. Emileigh and Aria were not sure what to make of it all.

Dinner was announced and we went to a buffet of salads, breads, desserts and meats. I even recognized most of the items. After dinner, a belly dancer appeared from the far end of the dining room. Mahmoud had thoughtfully made sure we had front row seats. Looking at John, I noticed he was doing an in-depth study of the tablecloth and chandelier. Our girls thought his discomfort was hilarious.

She shook her hips to every corner of the room to the video cameras which were now in use. As she exited, a whirling dervish leaped to the stage and began his dance of rapid spinning. Wearing a colorful skirt and cape, he twirled constantly while kicking, leaping and performing a variety of gravity-defying tricks.

In his final twirling a little man appeared from under the skirt of the dervish and also began twirling. He flipped and flapped to the oohs and aahs of the tourists. I was not sure if I should clap or be horrified.

The tall man twirled over to Aria to ask for a picture of them together. John smiled and shook his head "no." The dervish smiled and intimated to the audience that the women at our table were flowers and John was a devil. John said that was just fine.

Mahmud signaled us to follow him to the exit. The ship had docked, but he wanted to check to see if we wanted to personally meet the belly dancer and dervishes. We thanked him profusely, but assured him the show was more than enough.

He asked repeatedly if we enjoyed the program. We did indeed. Truly, we had never experienced anything like that. (We only have clogging in Missouri.)

He drove us back to our hotel and offered to take us to see the pyramids next. We were moved by his kindness. Yes, he did benefit from tourists, but he went beyond cursory politeness. Mahmoud genuinely wanted us to experience all the splendor of Egypt.

Little did we know that in a city of 23 million and no Arabic skills on our part, we would need every bit of kindness they had to offer.

Culture Cue

Invite an other-culture friend to a local event. He will appreciate the chance to explore his new surroundings while having a friend help him feel less intimidated.

3

Hamdee · Apartments and Landlords and Contracts, Oh My!
Navigate a New Culture, Trust People

Our language school had arranged for a local agent to help us find an apartment, or "flat" as Europeans say, in an area of the city we thought would put us in good proximity to our classes. We wanted to learn Arabic (fluently, of course!) before we began our work in education in Sudan.

The idea seemed straightforward. However, we had a tight timeline and the agent had a limited schedule, which combined, created a window of exactly 1 day to search, view, decide and secure said domicile.

This would be a daunting challenge for anyone anywhere, but the sheer magnitude of Cairo is overwhelming. Highrises sprawl as far as the eyes can see. Literally millions upon millions of people call this ancient city home. Now four sincere, but completely dependent Americans, were hoping to find some tiny nook among these people to call home. Impossible, except we had Hamdee.

Hamdee, our newly appointed agent, asked us to meet him at the school's office at 11 a.m. Me, raised by my parents' philosophy that if you are not 15 minutes early then you are late, arrived promptly with a slightly annoyed family at 10:45.

A smiling woman wearing a white turban-like headdress greeted us and asked us to take a seat as the agent would be "a few hours behind." Did she just say "hours"?

I did not realize that in that moment I was learning a lesson about time in the Middle East. Time is relative. 11 a.m. does not actually mean 11 a.m. It means sometime around that time or considerably later, someone will indeed come after all other social responsibilities have been met. Being "late" for an appointment is never discussed. We settled into our chairs and began playing thumb wars.

> **Now four sincere, but completely dependent Americans, were hoping to find some tiny nook among these people to call home.**

To our surprise, Hamdee, our agent arrived only 20 minutes after the "hours" remark. He greeted us warmly with a sturdy handshake for John and a nod in the direction of the girls and me. The purple, oval callous on his forehead indicated he was a devout Muslim who prayed five times a day by bowing and touching his head to the ground. He had a quick smile, need of some fattening and looked to be in his early 30s.

After pleasantries, he excitedly announced, "I have three beautiful flats for you to view today!" He motioned for us to follow him and soon we were in his car receiving an informal tour of the sites.

He parked on a quiet street off a main drag and pointed to a building's third floor. "That is where I am taking you!" He knew we were on a short timeline so he practically sprinted to the door and wanted us to do the same.

I am not sure what I expected. I had not really thought through the process of apartment hunting in a giant city. Our family had just moved out of a 4 bedroom home that backed up to a nature center. Deer and turkey were our neighbors. Trees surrounded us.

I put on my "I can do this" smile and walked in the door of the flat. Hamdee began recounting all of its attributes. John and the girls began exploring the rooms. Their exclamations of "beautiful" and "so cool" were helping my overall attitude.

I tried to make a mental inventory of things I thought should be in a furnished apartment, but I could not stop the dialog from rolling around in my head.

"Why are you looking at this, Pam? This is for people who are staying."

"C'mon, Pam! This is what you all dreamed about. Get with it!"

"This is all a big joke, yes? I mean people visit places like this, but no one actually lives here, right?"

"I could put up nice curtains, a few pictures..."

"Whatever you do, do not sign anything!"

My face reflected none of this as Hamdee proudly pointed out the vast amounts of storage closets. He had heard that foreigners love storage. He had not been misled. He concluded the tour reminding us that we had two more flats to view.

Flat #2 also had a beauty of its own, but the German landlord stood in the center of the living room the entire time with his arms folded and a scowl firmly fixed daring us to rent his apartment. Our tour ended quickly. I could not imagine asking him to come fix a leaky faucet.

Hamdee informed us that Flat #3's owner was not ready to receive us so he suggested we relax a bit and get some lunch. I found this a bit funny since he had us running to and from the earlier apartment viewings because of our tight schedule. But, you have got to roll with it.

He took us to the hotel and said he would return at 4:30 p.m. We ate at the Korean restaurant inside the hotel and discussed all we had seen and experienced. The internal conversation continued...

"Are you really in Egypt?"

"You realize that if you rent an apartment here, you have to stay, right?"

"Jesus, this was just one of those 'see if I would be obedient' tests, yes?"

I tried to reassure myself all the while portraying the confident veneer of a wife and mother who had it all together. No one was fooled.

We ate and then took a nap trusting that Hamdee would indeed return. Around 4:40 p.m. he called and said that Flat #3 was ready. We were greeted by an elegant Egyptian woman named Kareema.

She gave us a personal tour describing her art and furniture choices for each room. She was friendly, kind and gracious. Her pristine red lipstick that matched her taut, silk *hijab* (head covering) told me she was also organized and no-nonsense. Hamdee pulled John aside and said, "This is a nice woman. You will like living here."

The bedrooms were spacious, the furniture tastefully placed and the view of the city spectacular. However, let's be real. What did the bathroom look like? I had heard stories, all kinds of stories.

I peeked in and sighed. The bathroom had fixtures that I recognized. The toilet actually looked like a toilet. (That is not always a guarantee in this part of the world.) It came with a bonus *bidet*. I just hoped that was not French for "washing machine."

John, Emileigh and Aria smiled and nodded to indicate their approval of the flat. So we are really doing this?

We sat down for tea while Hamdee and Kareema spoke in fast Arabic, pausing once in a while to stop and smile at us. After tea, we went to Hamdee's car to discuss all the flats we had seen. It was unanimous that Kareema's flat would be our new home. We took a moment to give thanks to God for the flat, Hamdee and our new landlady, Kareema.

John and I signed a year's contract and were told we would be able to move in as soon as she had it cleaned. We were scheduled to attend a conference in another country, so we had no problem with that. She assured us she would have everything ready upon our return. As we left I caught myself saying, "I can't wait until we can get settled into our new home!" What had I done?

Culture Cue

Ask an other-culture friend to run errands with you. She will appreciate the one-on-one time and also learn where all of the good local stores are.

4

Kareema · When Hospitality Meets Digestion
Learn From Others, Be Flexible

Back from the conference, we anxiously arrived at our new flat. Aria walked in first and said, "Welcome home, Family!"

Emileigh noticed that we had fresh flowers on our table. John had somehow sniffed out a dessert left in the kitchen by Kareema. I was overwhelmed by her kindness.

We began rolling our bags to our room when we noticed that something was wrong with the wood flooring. Waves of buckled parquet ran across the entire living room floor. We were planning on calling Kareema to let her know we had arrived and to thank her for her kind gifts, but now we had to report the problem.

Flustered and livid, Kareema apologized profusely. She would get to the bottom of this. We had no doubt. An Arab woman on a mission is like an F-5 tornado looking for a trailer park.

The night before, a neighboring flat had a pipe burst which overflowed to ours and caused all the wood in the living room to buckle.

Kareema offered to put us in a hotel so that we would "not suffer so." We assured her that we could live there during the repairs, but thanked her for her thoughtfulness.

On the day we thought the repairmen were coming, we planned

to walk to McDonald's which was right down the street. Yes, Egypt, too, is "lovin' it."

Around 10 a.m. (still no workmen), we were getting a bit hungry so we thought we would eat half a peanut butter sandwich to tide us over until we could eat a real meal. By 11, we began pacing the room, trying to think of things to do. At noon, we began to practice our Arabic numbers and look out the window. By 12:30 p.m. we decided to watch, "Prince Caspian" in hopes that it would make the time pass quicker. We could hear parts of it, but the local *mullah* (Muslim pastor) began reading his sermon over the loudspeaker and the competition was fierce.

At 2:30 p.m., the phone rang and our landlady, Kareema, called and said she would pick us up at 3 for lunch. Lunch? We had not even eaten breakfast yet and still no workmen. Kareema arrived right on time; we met her outside since parking is absolutely impossible anywhere in Cairo.

We zipped to a stylish restaurant in an area close to our flat. It was called, "Spectra." Inside it looked just like any nice American restaurant. I relaxed a little.

Kareema felt so bad that our flat was not ready that she was going to nourish our damaged psyches with food and lots of it.

Her husband, Ali, had a table ready for us and directed us to sit. We smiled nervously as we could feel the persisting stares of the locals in the nearby booths.

Ali and Kareema's daughter, Alya, arrived taking her place next to me. She greeted us in brilliant English and suggested we look through the menu together. Each selection looked like good options, so we asked for a recommendation.

Kareema ordered for us, insisting that we eat our own dinner and not share. This posed a bit of a conundrum. We had just read earlier in the day in a home remedy book that when one has... well...intestinal issues, it is best to eat lightly so as to let one's internal organs rest. It was not to be.

Kareema felt so bad that our flat was not ready that she was going to nourish our damaged psyches with food and lots of it.

Our plates were brimming with veal, pasta and fresh veggies. My Diet Pepsi had ice (Huzzah!) and John tried a mint lemonade at their prodding. We ate and visited and ate and visited.

I'm thinking, *Don't say anything stupid. Be gracious. Say thank you. Ask questions, but don't be too invasive.* We were navigating these cultural waters safely and John did not give me any, "Luuuuuuuuuccccyyy!" looks. I felt good.

Ali asked the girls questions and chatted with them like a kind grandpa.

About an hour and a half passed since the meal had begun, and my current intestinal security system began signaling DEFCON 4. My organs needed rest and they needed it now. I pushed my plate forward a bit and began sipping my drink slowly.

The waiter came, took our plates and put the food in boxes for later. Fine. We were just about to thank our hosts for a lovely meal when dessert menus were thrust into our hands. I smiled a pained smile. As kindly as I could I told her I was very full and satisfied.

She smiled in return and asked if I wanted the "Oreo Madness" or strawberry cheesecake. I suggested that perhaps all three of us girls could share one dessert. She agreed since the desserts were normally large portions. I breathed a sigh of relief.

The waiter returned and she promptly ordered two "Oreo Madness" desserts and a slice of strawberry cheesecake. She looked at John, but he held his ground. He kindly told her that his lemonade drink would be dessert enough. She smiled and ordered him a second one.

Our desserts arrived but to the chagrin of our hosts the ice cream in the "Oreo Madness" bowls was the wrong flavor. The owner was embarrassed. He insisted we take the "wrong" ones and the quickly replaced "right" ones with his compliments. Now instead of three desserts we had five.

We were approaching the 2-hour mark when my digestive track had reached DEFCON 5. I whispered to Jesus asking Him to please not let this turn into an "incident" from which I would have to try and correct for the rest of the year.

Coffee and tea were offered, but we politely declined. They seemed satisfied with that. Our hosts motioned for us to leave so Ali and Alya said goodbye as Kareema led us to her car. She began the drive back to our flat but offered to take a different route to show us some of the features of our neighborhood.

I had small tears forming in the corners of my eyes, but I kept quoting "I can do all things through Christ who strengthens me" (Philippians 4:13, NIV). "Please, Digestive Tract, I won't mistreat you so ever again if only you can cooperate with me this time." (I heard a gurgling chuckle reverberating from my belly as if to say, "You speak with forked tongue.")

Finally, our tour ended and we finished our time together by paying her 6 months rent in advance. Most of the time it is customary to pay a year in advance, but Kareema assured us 6 months was good enough for now. We thanked her for such a wonderful time and waved goodbye. When she had driven a bit into the distance, I sprinted to the elevator to get to our flat on the 12th floor.

I put my key in the lock and attempted to unlock it. No go. I looked up at the number on the door to make sure that I had the right apartment. I did. I tried again. No go. My intestines are now at a countdown sequence, "Your stomach will self-destruct in 30, 29, 28…."

John and the girls had joined me by now. It dawned on us that the key that controls the deadbolt from the inside of the apartment must still be in the lock thus preventing us from entering from the outside.

Noooooooooooooooooooo!

I took one look at John and said, "One of the girls will go with me. One will stay with you. I'm heading to McDonald's." Emileigh and I bolted for the restaurant not really caring how it looked for two foreign woman to be running through the business district of Cairo.

I will not be indelicate, but I will just say that a crisis was averted, and I will forever bless the visionaries who insisted that McDonald's restaurants were needed around the world.

We returned to find John, Aria, our security guard and a locksmith all gathered around the doorknob. The locksmith had a sledge hammer, banging loudly trying to break the lock. We had wanted to meet our neighbors, but there had to be a better way.

After several hammers, looks of disapproval, grunts of trying and flying parts, we were in. The security guard smiled at us and allowed the women to enter while the men finished up. By the end, we had a new lock, four keys, full bellies and tabled digestive negotiations.

We looked around the flat and noticed that the workmen never did show up. When we were told "the day after Thursday," they actually meant Saturday. It was assumed that they would not come on Friday. Friday is not a workday for most people in the Middle East. Understood by everyone but the Morton family who sat for so long and waited for naught.

Thanks to Kareema and her over-the-top hospitality, we sensed our digestive tracts would not "work" on Fridays anymore either.

Culture Cue

Everyone longs for opportunities to connect with others no matter what culture he or she comes from. Taking time to sip and chat is a hallmark of many cultures across the world. Next time you see an other-culture person, invite her out for tea.

5

Ahmed · You Speak Tarzan?
Communicate, Learn Their Language

In the Disney animated cartoon, *Tarzan*, the lead character is orphaned in the jungle leaving him to be raised by gorillas. As an adult, he encounters a British woman who left England for the same jungle to follow her father who was researching wildlife. The famous interaction ensues, "I'm Tarzan," he says. She responds, "I'm Jane."

That describes our interactions during those first weeks in Cairo. Verbs were scarce, conjugations fleeting and sentences completed in charades. This made everyday life interesting to say the least.

John, however, took this Tarzan-like existence as a challenge to still try and make friends (loincloth excepted).

Every day after language school, he spoke to our building's security guards using the new words he had learned in class. One guard named Ahmed seemed to appreciate the attempt at communication. John would form a sentence such as, "I at school learn much. Your day good?"

Ahmed smiled and asked John to join him and his coworkers for tea. John sat on a little stool they pulled out for him and pressed on with the rest of the 38 Arabic words he knew–a bit odd since most were names of vegetables.

Several guards wearied of the stilted conversation and broke off into their own discussions. Ahmed continued to encourage John, giving him language tips and constantly saying, "You speak Arabic good!" John laughed and thanked him for his kindness.

I, on the other hand, preferred to illustrate my Arabic words with flamboyant hand gestures and exaggerated facial expressions. I felt that this added to the overall understanding of the hearer. The hearer doth not agree. Rather it seemed that it caused all the more confusion.

For instance, Ahmed, who had been so encouraging to John could not understand a simple question I had been asking him in what I would say was extremely articulate Arabic.

"Store grocery be where?" I asked.

"The what?" he replied.

"The store GRO-CER-Y," I enunciated.

He responded with a quizzical look that cued me to begin adding gestures and louder volume.

Verbs were scarce, conjugations fleeting and sentences completed in charades.

Flapping and waving while creating an invisible grocery store, I asked again, "BE WHERE STORE GRO-CER-Y?"

He was visibly confused, the girls horribly embarrassed and I painfully perturbed. I took a deep breath and was preparing another round of verbal calisthenics, when Emileigh touched my arm and said, "I got this."

She then very calmly asked him in beautiful sounding Arabic, "Sir, do you know where a grocery store is?"

Ahmed gave his biggest smile. "Yes! Yes! You speak good Arabic like your father." (I ignored that remark.)

He pointed to the street in front of our building and began giving a list of *yemeens* and *shemels* (rights and lefts). Emileigh nodded in acknowledgement, repeated the directions to Aria who is our human GPS system, and we were off like a shot.

As we walked toward the store, we had a good belly laugh. The girls reenacted my Tarzan performance, and we laughed again. We did find the store just as Ahmed had directed.

His kindness and patience allowed us to practice our new language and find jelly to go with our U.S. peanut butter. Chalk that up as a win for Tarzan.

Culture Cue

If you ask your other-culture friend a question, give him time to respond. Learning a new language is tough and processing answers takes a little longer. Encourage your friend to keep trying by smiling and affirming his efforts.

6

Nader · Koshary
Observe Common Practices,
Glean From Those Around You

When we first arrived in Cairo and began to unpack, Aria found a little book that a friend had given her entitled, *Cairo in Your Pocket*. This little book contained all kinds of interesting things that newcomers would want to know—which hotels to stay at, things to do, where to eat and even who had the best belly dancers. (We inadvertently found out about that already.) I looked through it again and found an ad for *koshary*. *Koshary* is a popular dish that originates from Egypt's 10 percent Coptic Orthodox Christian community.

The Coptics needed something that would still be a filling combination of foods that did not include meat or dairy during Lent—thus, *koshary* was created. One restaurant in particular advertised heavily that their *koshary* was the best in Cairo. We thought it might be a fun outing to find this place and try it... though we were probably poor judges because we had never had bad *koshary* or any *koshary*, but nonetheless.

Of course, John poured over the maps, got a plan and told the girls it was time for lunch and a geography lesson. We were going to take a taxi to a Metro station (subway) and then ride the Metro the rest of the way to the restaurant. This had worked before.

We hopped in a taxi (a new one with the plastic still on the seats) and began darting through traffic. We drove for quite a while when I realized we were not anywhere close to the Metro station we had used before. In fact, he drove and drove and drove. We crossed a bridge over a body of water and John whispered, "We might as well have him take us to the restaurant. We're almost there anyway."

Thankfully, we still had our pocket guide and we showed him the picture of the ad. He nodded, rolled his eyes and said, "You want go there now?" John said, "*Iowa*" ("Yes").

The man murmured about the traffic, drove a bit longer and finally dropped us off at a corner of a busy side street.

We looked at the sign that said, "*Abou Tarek: Koshary*." Another sign said, "This is the only branch." I am not sure why it said that, but maybe it reflected a failed expansion or competition around the city.

Heads turned as we were the only non-everythings in the restaurant.

Heads turned as we were the only non-everythings in the restaurant. The cashier motioned for us to go upstairs. We found a table for four next to two women in a corner of the almost full room. One of them smiled at me as we sat down. I cannot wait until I can actually say something more than "Hello" and recite my Arabic numbers 1-10.

A waiter introduced himself as Nader and asked us what we wanted. John said, "*Koshary*." Nader asked if we wanted four orders. John nodded. Then he asked us what we wanted to drink. We told him.

He returned a few minutes later and began talking to John (in Arabic). John said, "I don't understand." He repeated it. John said, "I'm sorry. I still don't understand." This continued back and forth like a bad ping pong game until the waiter went back downstairs.

Nader came with a tray of drinks. He handed us four bottles of water. I had asked for a Diet Pepsi or Diet Coke, but I got water. I have learned it is better just to take whatever they bring you. We sipped on our water and took in the sights through the window that looked out at the traffic below. Arab men were talking with one another. People were purchasing, selling and carrying their goods.

My thoughts were interrupted when our waiter set four steel bowls on our table. Each bowl came with its own small pitcher of sauce. He pointed at a tall pitcher on our table and said, "Spicy." We said a prayer of thanks and began to dive in. This was carb heaven in a bowl...rice, spaghetti, chickpeas, lentils, fried onions and some unidentifiable spices. The little pitcher of sauce tasted like the kind you would put on spaghetti. John got adventurous and tried the "spicy" pitcher. He breathed fire for 10 minutes and thoroughly fried his tastebuds. I decided that I would pass.

We offered the girls each 5 Egyptian pounds if they would try it. Emileigh said the exchange rate was not worth the pain.

We agreed it was quite delicious and very filling. As we were finishing up, I noticed a sign in a corner written in English. It read, "Please pay first." Oh, so that is what the waiter had been trying to tell us. Oh, well. Next time. We put the extra in a takeaway box, paid our bill and said goodbye to Nader.

He smiled and told us in broken English, "You welcome any time!" We learned a little bit more today and had a great meal. Nader served us even though we did not follow any of the known processes. Who knew we would need help to even eat in a restaurant? Nader did and he came through.

Culture Cue

If you see an other-culture person at a restaurant dining or working, take a moment to introduce yourself. It is quite common in other cultures to welcome foreigners in any venue.

7

Mohammad · Taxi Politics
Listen to His Story First, Understand an Opinion

Public transportation in Cairo is plentiful and cheap—usually. One of the biggest stresses I faced had been securing a taxi, describing the destination and haggling a fair price. Emileigh found this exercise exhilarating; I found it three levels more difficult than returning an unwanted Christmas gift at Wal-Mart on December 26.

The girls and I had heard about a mall across town that boasted all things recognizable—Chili's, Applebee's, Hallmark and more. We had been living other-culture for almost three months and felt the need for something, anything familiar. This seemed to be the ticket.

We stood on the corner by our flat waiting for a newer taxi to pass. ("Newer" because I prefer latches on doors and windows with glass.) Soon a driver pulled up and the bargaining dance began. I described where we wanted to go and he nodded through the whole description.

"Yes! Yes! I take you!" he exclaimed.

Once I had been convinced he actually knew where we wanted to go, I asked about the price.

"Good price. Good price. Anything you want. For free even!" he said in English.

I laughed, "No, seriously, how much?"

"My name is Mohammad. Anything you want! You are guest in Egypt!" He stretched and opened the back door.

I looked at the girls and shrugged. "Let's give it a try." They looked dubious, but got in.

He accelerated while muttering a variety of Arabic phrases that seemed to be for the fellow drivers who were impeding his progress. I had not learned those yet. Probably all the better.

He turned up the volume on the radio. I immediately recognized what was playing. He had a recording of a man reciting the Qur'an. In order for him to hear it well in the front, he had to blare the speakers from the back where we were sitting.

It was loud and I was annoyed. I caught a reflection of Mohammad in the rear view mirror. About 40 years old, he wore the traditional *tageeya* (Muslim hat) and bore a callous on his forehead from bowing five times a day in prayer. His chin strap beard stretched below his collar.

He yelled over the sound, "Where are you from?"

"We are from America," I said.

"Oh, Obama good!" he smiled.

I had been advised to remain apolitical in all discussions foreign and domestic. One simply never knew where the subject was headed.

I smiled and said, "We like Egyptian people very much."

I paused and wondered at my own zeal.

Mohammad continued in English, "Why America make trouble for us? America should follow Islam. You Muslim?"

Again tap-dancing ever so carefully I said, "We have enjoyed our time in Egypt. The people are so kind. We are Christians."

He clucked his tongue and said, "You can be Muslim! I teach you!"

I was getting nervous. He seemed agitated, and I did not have a GPS body tracker like all good special ops people wear. I began to pray.

"Why you not be Muslim? Do you not love our prophet?"

I did not have enough Arabic to have a thorough discussion and his English was not far enough along for an involved response from me. Heck, I do not have enough Arabic to tell him to stop this car immediately and let us out. I began gathering options when I saw the mall appear in the distance.

"There it is!" I shouted.

"Yes! Yes! I know where it is," he said.

Relieved that our conversation was coming to a close, I began pulling out Egyptian pounds to pay him. I really have no idea what is proper and his meter (as is fairly usual) did not work. I handed him a bill and he nodded. Rats. That meant that I had paid too much. However, I was in no mood to argue.

As we piled out, Mohammad tried one more time, "You should be Muslim!"

We waved goodbye and breathed a prayer for this man so zealous for all to know his god. He had made his beliefs very clear. I paused and wondered at my own zeal. Did I take every opportunity? Did I want to? Did I even think to?

Culture Cue

Invite an other-culture friend to go with you to a religious service. Many times other-culture people are interested in the beliefs of their host country.

8

Hedra, George & Yusef · Now You're Cookin'
Open Your Home, Build Deeper Relationships

Three of our Egyptian friends (who also are brothers) asked if it would be okay if they came to our house and cooked for us. Let me get this straight...

You want to come to our house.

You will buy the groceries and bring them.

You cook an entire meal for us.

We will eat authentic Egyptian dishes.

That is an incredibly kind offer. For a woman such as myself, who is constantly trying to come up with new and exciting culinary items based on three ingredients...amazing.

I took a dignified 1.2 seconds before shouting, "Of course!"

We had met the brothers through a mutual friend and instantly connected. They were like long-lost (non-pasty) cousins that we were introduced to at a family reunion. Hedra taught us about Egyptian culture. George helped us with Arabic, errands and finding delicious restaurants. Shy Yusef, the youngest, had a special skill in cooking.

They arrived around 3 p.m. carrying bags of various produce and meat. Two of the three brothers (Hedra and George) headed into the living room. Yusef happily began organizing the items needed for the menu. I gave a kitchen orientation and scooted out. It was a one-cook-sized kitchen.

I found out later that Hedra's role was to purchase the food, while George helped with cleanup.

Soon delicious smells wafted into the sitting area. For once I did not have to say, "Boy, someone in our apartment building is cooking something really great!" This time it was us.

Yusef worked while George helped John again with some Arabic homework. The rest of us entertained ourselves with stories, schooling and a pre-dinner cookie or two. I would poke my head into the kitchen, asking the chef a question or two about the ingredients, and then leave him to his duties.

Finally, Yusef announced that dinner was ready. We sat down and John prayed a prayer of thanks.

I took a dignified 1.2 seconds before shouting, "Of course!"

Soon scoops of rice and baked chicken were being passed between all of us. Other dishes (which I cannot remember the names) were included, too. John commented that this was the best Egyptian food we had eaten since arriving months before. It was true. Yusef had outdone himself.

We all pretty much licked the platters clean and then talked about how good everything was one more time. I served ice cream afterward as it "helps fill in the cracks," according to a friend from Alabama.

Following dinner we began rounds of "Hot Seat." Our daughters taught us this game. Someone sits in the "hot seat" and becomes the focus of the group. The group then asks all kinds of random questions in order to find out more about the person. Some questions can be as simple as, "What's your favorite color?" while others more confusing like, "If a taco and a grilled cheese got in a fight, who would win?"

We laughed at some of the questions and responses. Without realizing it, we had come up on 11 p.m. We teased Yusef because we had eaten at 7:30 p.m. which is not too far past the Egyptians' normal lunchtime. We asked him if he were going to start dinner soon.

Of course, the "nursing home" hosts were finished and had school the next day, so we did not require any more cooking for the evening. Although I did ask if he were available during Ramadan, the month when Muslims fast during daylight and feast in the evenings.

Around midnight we said our goodbyes, thanking the Lord for these kind Christian brothers He had placed in our path. Though Egypt is 90 percent Muslim, there is a small but growing population of evangelical Christians. Hedra, George and Yusef are a part of this group.

Their kindness and encouragement have helped us on our most difficult days when dear family and friends are so far away. We fell into a deep food-induced sleep, preparing ourselves mentally for another day of learning Arabic.

I closed with this prayer:
"Lord,
May the chicken in my belly
Nourish the words in my brain.
Bless all that I am learning
And let my tongue not get a sprain.
Amen."

Culture Cue

Invite your other-culture friend over for a holiday meal. He will appreciate being included, learning about your culture and the feeling of belonging.

9

Ada · Goat Parts, Part 1
Understand Better, Go to Their Home

Arabic is and will remain a lifelong pursuit of understanding. I chuckle when I am asked, "When will you
be fluent?"

"The 22nd of never," I reply.

It is tough. Really tough. It ranks as one of the most difficult
languages in the world to learn for English speakers. Still, if we
want to serve the dear people in this part of the world, then it
makes sense that we would speak in the language of their heart.
Currently, I am speaking the language of their 2-year-old hearts.

John and I attended a formal language school 4 days a week.
Emileigh and Aria were enrolled in classes across town that fit
with their online homeschool schedule. On paper, it seemed quite
manageable and reasonable.

I told John that, if I ever had a serious illness and am given a
short time to live, I know what I will do. I will enroll in language
school because whatever time I have left will feel like the longest
days of my life.

However, teachers like Ada made this process of being 40-year-
old toddlers so much easier. In her late 20s, Ada wore a *hijab*, a
quick smile and a no-nonsense attitude. She had taught foreigners

for a while and was keen to all their excuses and rationales for their inability to learn Arabic.

She was an excellent teacher and had become a good friend. Following one of our month-long sessions, Ada invited us to her family's home for a meal. We were honored.

We had not received an invite like this before so we did not know what to expect. I knew she was a conservative Muslim though she did not wear the *niqab* (face veil). How this played out in a home setting, I was not sure.

I baked cookies and presented them to her when we arrived at her door at 6 p.m. She ushered us into a small family room that had Qur'an quotes in gold hung on the walls. We sat on velvet couches and were given glasses of fresh-squeezed orange juice.

> **We had not received an invite like this before so we did not know what to expect.**

Ada excused herself from the room, leaving us alone. We smiled at each other and breathed a prayer of blessing over this family. Soon she returned and pointed to the dining area.

"It's ready!" she said in brilliant English.

We sat down at the table that had five chairs around it. Dishes of food covered the surface completely. I remarked at the beautiful food which seemed to please Ada immensely.

We waited for her to sit as well, but she did not. She began scooping helpings onto our plates. Still we waited to eat, thinking she would soon sit.

"Eat! Eat!" she said.

So we did. I tried to make conversation by asking the names of the different dishes, but their names were in Arabic so it did not really mean a lot to me. I nodded politely and tried to eat equal amounts of everything.

After our plates were filled to her satisfaction, she disappeared.

"Ah, she must be getting her family now to join us," I said.

More minutes passed and no Ada. We continued eating and chatting.

Ada ran back in asking, "Do you like? Do you like?"

We all nodded, exclaiming how good everything tasted.

"My mother helped me make everything," she said.

"Please tell her that it is all very delicious," John said.

This made her extremely happy. So happy in fact that she said, "You must eat more!"

We had already eaten a lot. I mean a lot. In America, it is polite to clean your plate to show the hostess that the food was good. In Egypt, it was a sign that you had not had your fill. (We did not know this at that time, though.) We had done this to ourselves.

She brought out more dishes from the kitchen (seriously?) and scooped new items on our plate. Once more, she disappeared and we reviewed our plates.

"Is this *mahshi?*" Aria asked.

"It could be," I replied. It did have the look of a small zucchini stuffed with rice.

Emileigh popped it in her mouth and said, "It's good."

I tasted it as well and knew instantly that this was no zucchini. It had a strange texture. Still I was committed in that moment.

Ada returned and I asked her to tell me about the new dishes. She pointed at different ones until she got to the zucchini-looking bowl. She said the name to which of course I did not know.

John asked a follow-up question and he began to smile, almost suppressing a laugh.

Being a great Egyptian hostess, she filled our plates a third time even though we still had food remaining from Round 2. She excused herself to prepare dessert.

John had tears in his eyes now as he could not hold back any longer.

"What's so funny?" I asked.

"You know those zucchini things we've been eating?" he asked now, shaking like a paint-mixer from trying to laugh silently.

"Yes, what did she say it is?"

"It's goat," he responded, cryptically.

"Okay, goat what?"

Emileigh immediately began laughing hysterically though quietly. Aria and I sat transfixed. "Goat what?" I asked again.

"You have a plate full of male goat parts stuffed with rice!"

My brain could not calculate what he was saying. Male, what? Goat, what? Stuffed where?

Now all three are laughing as they watch the questioning drain from my face and refill with a shocking understanding.

How can I possibly eat this knowing what I know? Ignorance truly is bliss.

Ada poked her head in and said, "You must eat so we can have dessert!"

My brain could not calculate what he was saying. Male, what? Goat, what? Stuffed where?

I knew we needed to honor the hostess by eating what she had prepared. I also knew my arm was numb, making the use of my fork implausible.

Emileigh piped up, "I'll eat your goat parts if you finish my soup!"

Soup for goat parts? What blessed child is this I have? "Deal!"

We quickly passed around the varieties of food until we felt as if we had made a good showing of culinary intake.

Ada seemed pleased and began taking our half-eaten plates away to her family who was sitting in the kitchen preparing to eat what remained.

Tea and dessert were served signaling the end of our visit. I was not sure I would be able to physically lift myself from the couch. I do not remember eating that much food ever even on Thanksgiving.

We thanked Ada profusely for her kindness, her good cooking and her warm hospitality. As we were in the taxi back to our flat, we groaned at our full bellies and laughed at all the parts we had consumed in the last 2 hours.

Aria said, "Well, I'll certainly have something interesting to write in my journal tonight!"

Culture Cue

When you make a favorite dish, take a small plate of it over to your other-culture neighbor. In many cultures, sharing plates of food between families is common and a good way to create a friendship.

10

Abdu · Adopted Friend
Look for Teachers, Be Ready to Learn

Abdu, a taxi driver, adopted us. We did not realize this until he asked during our first ride how long language classes lasted. We told him. When classes were finished, he was waiting for us. The next morning he was at our apartment. This continued during our entire stay in Cairo.

In his 40s, Abdu was a former office manager who was trying to care for his family by driving a taxi until a new job opened up. He greeted us every morning, "Hello, Mr. Zhan (John)!" He then smiled at the girls and me while opening the car door for us.

He wore office clothes every day because, "I am an office manager. I must not forget!" Driving a taxi is not a prestigious job, but he did it for his family. He did not seem so different from our friends in the U.S. facing the same situation.

He rushed around to the driver's seat and began asking about our Arabic studies. He spoke fairly good English, so we could converse between the two languages. As he would drive, he would point to things and tell us the Arabic word for them. Then he would have us repeat them. He could cram a lot of words in a 10-minute ride. After class, he would quiz us about our lessons. At stoplights and traffic jams, he looked at John's notes and handouts and asked questions. John must then respond with the proper Arabic response.

He had Arabic letters written down for us to recite when we got in the car. He was happy to teach us and said that he "doesn't even charge us any moneys."

One day as we were exiting the taxi, he asked John to stay. Abdu began telling him more about his wife and children. He ended with, "You my friend."

John asked if he could pray a prayer of blessing on his family. Abdu nodded yes. With tears in his eyes, Abdu said, "I feel your heart. No one pray for me like this before."

John answered, "God will help you, Abdu. I will continue to pray." Abdu responded with a traditional Muslim response, "*Insh'allah. Insh'allah.*" ("If God wills it.")

He did not seem so different from our friends in the U.S. facing the same situation.

We appreciated Abdu's friendship. We relied on his consistent work ethic, and we trusted him to drive our girls around the city even when we were not with them. He adopted us, but we had adopted him, too.

Culture Cue

Take time to really listen to your other-culture friend. Ask questions. Be compassionate.

11

Aemed · Farm Visit–The First 11 Hours
Forget Your Watch, Be Present

Living in Cairo felt like the tipping point at the peak of a 360° roller coaster. Twists and turns, dips and highs... times when I was sure no one could possibly survive such a ride. But somehow, Arabic grew, relationships formed and friendships deepened.

John spent a lot of time with our security guards in the afternoon and evening. He was regularly invited to sit, drink tea and chat. One guard invited our entire family to his home for dinner. We accepted and the preparations began, but I was anxious about the whole event. I had reasons:

1. I did not know any of these people.
2. We were going to a village far from the city for the first time.
3. What if I create an international incident with perceived unseemly behavior?
4. America does not negotiate with terrorists.
5. What if goat parts are the only thing on the menu?

I shared my concerns with the family in a more rational and logical way. They met my concerns with smiles, a pat on the shoulder and Aria quipping, "Oh, Marms..." They obviously had an extra "adventure" gene in their DNA.

Aemed (Eye-med) told us he lived 1.5 hours away from our home so plans had to be made for securing transport. We would leave with Aemed when he got off work, take a taxi to the mini-bus station, take said mini-bus to his village and then catch a micro-bus to his farm. Micro-busses in Cairo are affectionately called, "Flying Coffins." Following that evening, I had four cases of empirical evidence to corroborate this.

In a normal vehicle, on a normal road, at a normal speed Aemed probably lived closer to 2.5 hours away. But since breaking the sound barrier seemed to be important to most Egyptian drivers, we made it in the time predicted.

Still white-knuckled from the bus ride, we came to a screeching halt in front of Aemed's apartment building.

Some kids who were playing around a tree immediately began staring at us. They were joined by a few farm workers. Aemed had to inform the curious neighbors who we were as he ushered us down the middle of the now-growing crowd to his home.

Aemed proudly motioned for us to go into the living room. We sat down and took in our surroundings: simple concrete structure, peach painted walls, dark green velvet chairs and a few gold framed Qur'an verses on the wall. Aemed told us, "Take a resty" and turned on the TV. He adjusted his satellite dish and smiled when he found *Gladiator* on. He said, "I love Russell Crowe."

He left the room and we relaxed a little. We smiled at each other and stared at the TV. He brought John and me slippers because we could not be cool until we took off our socks and shoes and wore sandals. Next, Mama came in. She was the family matriarch and as sweet as can be. She spoke no English and could barely hear Arabic.

Aemed went to check on his wife. I asked her a few questions, but realized by her blank stare we were getting no where. Aemed came in soon in a white *jalabaya* (man's robe) and bare feet. We returned to Russell Crowe, as he stood in the arena fighting for his life while thousands of onlookers watched. I felt a strange kinship.

I then chuckled inwardly and thought, *Well, this is not how I pictured this visit. That is for sure. Maximus made it through and so will we!*

This life was making me weird.

I was thirsty after our long ride, but did not want to pull out my water bottle and risk offense. I waited. I was growing impatient. Before the evening was over, Aemed and his family were going to show me that offered drinks were never going to be forgotten.

Aemed then announced that dinner was ready. He led us to a beautifully set table laden with Egyptian delicacies. I saw no obvious goat parts. Aemed motioned for us to sit and left the room.

We waited for him, his wife and Mama to come join us, but they did not. We sat in silence with our hands politely folded wondering what to do.

He returned to the room and began flapping his arms.

"Why aren't you eating?" he asked. We told him we were waiting for his family.

He said, "No, no, no! Eat! Eat!"

He then picked up each bowl and give us what he thought was an appropriate amount to eat. Aria was closest to him, so she would get double the amount.

He watched us eat for a while and then said, "Egyptians don't eat like that. We use our hands." I was just cutting something with my knife and fork and looked at him. He then said, "It's okay. It's okay."

He sat down for a few minutes and began to eat. Between bites, he placed more food on our plates, since they had dipped below a foot tall.

When he left the room again, Emileigh passed some of her food onto John's plate. She said, "I'm going to explode if I eat any more food!" We could not stop laughing. The food was good, but we could not even make a dent in the amount.

Aemed returned and gave Aria some more food. We knew that Aria, too, was beyond her intake amount. We tried to distract him from serving us more by asking the name of each dish and telling him how good everything was.

His wife came and we thanked her for such a beautiful meal. She disappeared again and Aemed was standing for another round of food dishing. John thanked him but told him he could eat no more. They bantered back and forth until Aemed said, "In Egypt, when you are full you say, 'I have a full tank.'"

John laughed, rubbed his stomach and said, "I definitely have a full tank." Aemed seemed satisfied with that. We washed our hands and returned to the living room.

Russell Crowe was still fighting in Rome. Mama was still in the chair now holding a baby. Aemed and his wife were the proud parents of a 5-month-old girl and grandma was now cradling her. We took turns holding her and congratulating the proud papa. He was beaming.

Soon sisters, brothers, uncles, nieces, nephews, cousins began filtering in at a pace that prevented me from keeping up with who's who. All of them scooted into the small living room and smiled. We smiled back. They smiled some more. We asked the few things we could in Arabic and prayed under our breath that Aemed would wander back into the room soon to translate.

Before we made the trek to their home, we had purchased an Arabic to English dictionary. So John sat with his English to Arabic dictionary in his lap and Aemed and the rest of his family held the other. Flipping through the pages created many opportunities for humor and a nice breeze.

Bananas were offered and we made a feeble attempt to decline. Mama would only be satisfied if we each ate one, but would have been happier if we had taken two. So we ate our bananas. The family watched.

Aemed worked in the city, but most of his family were farmers. They tilled a simple plot that grew beans and tomatoes providing a small subsistence income. Education and opportunities were limited. So were interactions with foreigners. Everything we did was met with fascination and curiosity.

I had brought along a children's picture book and asked one of the children to tell me what each picture was in Arabic. Aemed thought he could do a better job of it so he took the book from the child and began pointing out each picture. I was not really trying to learn in that moment, but rather pass the time and engage with some other family members.

Aemed invited us to go out on the balcony to see the fields behind his building. We enjoyed the view and sat in the palm-frond woven chairs provided. The family peeked around the balcony door and watched us watching the field workers. Soon a tray with tall glasses was set before us. Aemed's wife had prepared cantaloupe juice.

We drank the juice, enjoyed the scenery and played with the kids. John and Emileigh held a "How to Make an Origami Crane" session which seemed to be a hit. Cranes were passed to each child and they skipped away to show their parents. (One exception was the 3-year-old girl who threw hers over the balcony.)

An hour passed and another beverage came. This one was hot and had milk, rice, banana, hazelnuts and cinnamon. Any other time it would have been delicious, but after all that we had eaten I could only pray, "Lord, help me to get this down and keep it down." Aria and Emileigh eyes were pleading, but we could offer no help.

Welcome to your new life, Pam. Welcome to your new metaphoric life.

As the sun began to set, we were invited to tour the fields. We walked with Aemed, his older sister and three little friends. We walked passed wheat, orange trees, beans and tomato plants. The call to prayer was heard through the village and the sun began to set. We were walking back toward the house when we came upon Aemed's uncle sitting near a small fire in one of the corners of the field.

The uncle invited us to sit and drink tea. Another beverage. We sat on a mat while he boiled the tea. He handed John the first cup of hot steaming, sweet, black tea. He found another glass with a piece missing, but proceeded to prepare some tea for me. We drank in the dark and listened as Aemed translated for his uncle. "He has much happiness in his heart that you have come."

John and I finished our tea. The uncle took the cups, rinsed them out at the pump and fixed two more glasses for the girls. They finished their tea, and he prepared two more cups for himself and Aemed. It was dark outside by now. I thought, *How am I going to avoid all the animal deposits with no light?* Welcome to your new life, Pam. Welcome to your new metaphoric life.

Aemed led John and the girls back to the house. I was a bit behind trying to avoid stepping in "farm things" and found myself surrounded by a group of women from the village. I was redirected to one of Aemed's brother's apartment on a lower level. The rest of the family was missing. I now was with a whole new side of the family. No one seemed panicked but me. I breathed a prayer, hoping this was not the start of a *24* episode and followed the women into a living room.

BaBa (Grandpa) was sitting in the corner on a mat also watching Russell and smoking a *hookah*. He smiled a toothless smile and shook my hand. I tried my best Arabic greeting and he seemed pleased. The women took me to the other room of this two-room apartment and told me to sit. I sat and waited. They talked nonstop Arabic, pausing only for me to nod my head and watch me drink orange soda. The conversation (I think) went like this:

"I like America. We should go together. I want to go there."

(Pam looks like she doesn't understand because most likely she does not.)

"I like Sharm Elsheikh (vacation spot in Egypt). We should go together. I want to go there."

(Pam looks like she still does not understand.)

"Cairo is too far. You sleep here tonight. You stay with us."

(Pam resists the push on her shoulder to lie down and go to sleep right then.)

"We have bed. You sleep here."

We chatted back and forth. It probably was not as long as I thought; but when your language is so limited, it really shortens conversations and lengthens pauses. They were gracious to forgive my mistakes and help me with any word I was trying to think of. The women patted me some more, still tried to get me to lie down on the bed and go to sleep and hold their babies.

Finally I said, "My husband is looking for me. I need to go to him now. Thank you so much."

I heard someone yelling from the other apartment and one

hostess yelled back. Apparently, John had just told Aemed that he wanted me to come back to the house so they were making the transfer.

I gave John a knowing nod and mouthed, "Thank you."

We were reunited in Aemed's living room. This time there were even more family members. At the peak of the visit, I counted 26 in a room that would typically seat seven. The two dictionaries were still being passed back and forth when fresh spearmint tea was offered.

I heard that when one is in pain there comes a point when the pain is so great one stops feeling it. My stomach had reached that level. I drank the tea on autopilot and enjoyed our time with this warm, loving accepting family.

They did not seem to mind our feeble attempts at Arabic conversation. They were content for us to be together. One of Aemed's friends announced that we were the first Americans he had ever met in person. We tried to spend time talking with each visitor.

Another round of tea came. This was the kind the uncle had served earlier in the field. Six glasses still with stickers were on a tray. The family insisted we take our cups first. We tried to offer them some, but they would have none of it. After we drank the tea, the glasses were taken back to the kitchen, rinsed and refilled for six more members of the family.

Finally, Aemed asked us if we were ready to go back to Cairo. I almost jokingly said, "What? So soon?" but I did not for fear that they would make up the bed right then. We asked if we could take a family photo. They agreed and each began lining up for their photo op with the Mortons. We passed around the digital camera showing them the results.

As we hugged and said goodbye, each requested a photo so they could "hang it on their wall by Baba's picture."

We were so humbled by their kindness, acceptance and amazing generosity. They had little, but what they had they shared extravagantly.

Mama invited us to return and told us we were now family. We loaded into the micro-bus as the entire family stood beside it and waved goodbye. Aemed and his brother saw us to the "Flying Coffin" station where our driver took us and 12 other passengers back to Cairo with lightning speed.

Aemed called us on our cell to make sure we had arrived home safely. We thanked him again for such a wonderful evening. We went to sleep around midnight, thanking the Lord for allowing us the opportunity to make new friends and learn more about these sweet Egyptians.

Aria commented, "I'm not going to eat for three days."

Emileigh said, "You got that right!"

I agree, Aria. I agree.

Culture Cue

Surprise your other-culture friend by learning a greeting in her heart language. She will be thrilled to know you took the time to learn something about her culture.

12

Rafita · Farewell to Cairo
Seize Opportunities, Grow Friendships

Down the street from our flat, McDonald's served as our "branch office" throughout our time in Cairo because of its free wi-fi and my propensity for fountain Diet Cokes.

Outside the restaurant, red and yellow mopeds lined the curb ready to deliver imported Western-fried goodness to Egyptians desiring to remain out of the constant traffic fray. Inside, it looks like any typical McDonald's you might find in the States.

Throughout our visits, the workers always welcomed us warmly while practicing their best English.

"Welcome to McDonald's. May...I...take...your...order?" one employee asked proudly.

"I hope you are enjoyed," said another.

One manager, Rafita, took extra care each time we visited. She would stop by our table and ask if we liked our food. She offered to give us directions to places. At times, she brought the girls cookies because she "liked them too, too much."

In her early 30s, Rafita, a devout Muslim, longed to please God and pondered her place in life. She was, however, a bit of an anomaly in Egyptian culture. She is single, working outside the home and wants to explore the world.

We really liked her. She was fun, bright, and outgoing. Whenever we would visit McDonald's (for relationship, of course, had nothing to do with their *fried* apple pies. Yes, they still fry them in Egypt!), we would ask for her. She especially liked spending time with Emileigh and Aria. Friendship grew, but it was now time for us to say goodbye.

In a few days we would move on to Khartoum, Sudan. We explained to Rafita that we would relocate to work at a school. She nodded in understanding, but tears formed in her eyes.

I was moved by her deep emotions. I was not sure what to feel in the moment. We experienced so many different emotions throughout the year in Cairo, extreme highs and devastating lows. We navigated a completely new culture, learned some of its language, gathered social cues and established sincere friendships.

> **At times, she brought the girls cookies because she "liked them too, too much."**

I turned to Rafita and placed my hands on her shoulders. In my best Arabic I said, "Thank you, Rafita, for all your kindness. Thank you for loving my daughters. Thank you for all the free cookies. I pray that Jesus will bless you and your family in all you do, and I hope that you do get to explore the whole world."

I hugged her and prayed that somehow someway she understood the intent of my grammatical phrasings. She smiled and said, "*Shukron gazeelun!*" ("Thank you very much!")

She hugged Emileigh and Aria and nodded toward John. As we were leaving, she stood with the other employees as they all began to wave while shouting, "Goodbye! Thank you! We love you! Goodbye!"

Goodbye, Cairo!

Goodbye, Mark and Mahmoud!

Goodbye, Hamdee!

Goodbye, Kareema!

Goodbye, Ahmed!

Goodbye, Nader!

Goodbye, Mohammad!
Goodbye, Hedra, George and Yusef!
Goodbye, Ada!
Goodbye, Abdu!
Goodbye, Aemed!
Goodbye, Rafita!

Thank you for your love, your kindness, your challenges and your amazing hospitality. May Jesus be ever near you in your mind, your life and your family.

Culture Cue

Imagine yourself as an other-culture person. What does your new world look like through a different culture lens? Ask your other-culture friend something he has noticed that he finds unexpected.

Part 2:
The City • Khartoum, Sudan

13

Howwa · Be My Friend
Go Below the Surface, Ask Questions

One year after leaving the U.S. To move to Egypt, our family packed up our 28-tote lives and landed in Khartoum, Sudan. We would put down roots, live with the people, work in an international school and hope to Sweet Baby Moses that we would not self-combust from the heat.

Khartoum, a city of 8 million people, has been called "The World's Largest Village." I did not understand that until we began exploring our new city and discovered it was nothing like Cairo. Khartoum has a much more laid-back feel in part because of the soaring temperatures—but also the nature of the people.

The Sudanese welcome strangers with open smiles and invitations to drink tea together. Relationships meant more than time so watches were not necessary.

Eager to be someone's new best friend, I began introducing myself to any woman I could make eye contact with. I could be perceived as somewhat "enthu-

Relationships meant more than time so watches were not necessary.

siastic," but these women did not realize I was potentially the most sincere friend they might ever have if only given the chance.

An entire week had passed and I still had not found my "bosom friend." Feeling a bit out of sorts from my friendless state, the girls and I decided to take a drive through downtown. As we drove down one of the main roads, we noticed every so often a woman sitting under a tree with little stools around her.

We were intrigued. What is she doing? We could not guess.

We decided to stop and ask. We parked the truck and began walking toward a distinguished looking woman in her 50s. She wore a bright yellow *thobe* (cloth) around her and had her hands resting calmly on her lap.

She smiled as Aria greeted her in Arabic. Emileigh kissed the woman's cheeks and she directed us to sit on the stools. I told her that we were new in the city. She welcomed us and began fussing over a table of ingredients that she had in jars.

"We must drink tea!" she said.

"Oh, you sell tea?" I asked.

"Yes, yes. But you will not pay. You are my guest."

She turned her attention toward her small metal table which had a single propane burner and a tea kettle. She placed tea leaves along with cardamom, ginger, cloves and mint into a strainer and let the hot water pour over the mixture.

The tea had wisps of steam emerging from the traditional, small handleless glass cups. Taking a jar of sugar, she used her spoon to put three perfectly rounded heaps into each cup. Yay! She likes Southern-style sweet tea!

Once she completed the process, she put the glasses on a small silver tray and walked over to each one of us. She cautioned us to hold the glass at the rim and bottom edge so as not to burn ourselves. She then told us that once you can hold the cup with your hand, it is ready to drink. Clever.

We asked our gracious hostess what her name was.

"Howwa," she said, "I have five children. My husband is dead. I make money by selling tea."

Emileigh and Aria asked and answered questions as we sat under the shade of a tree.

I took in this scene. A middle-class American woman and her

two daughters sitting under a tree on a main street in Khartoum sipping tea with a sweet woman named Howwa. I felt so privileged.

We visited a few more minutes and then thanked her for her thoughtful hospitality.

"You must come back!" she said.

"We will, Howwa," I assured her. You don't know it yet, but we're about to become good friends.

Culture Cue

Your other-culture friend may highly value time together and visits in her home. Make time for a relaxed visit to your other-culture friend's home.

14

Ehab · Chipping Away at Culture
Forget Prediction, Assume Nothing

"I can't believe it!" my friend muttered.

"What's going on?" I asked.

She shook her head and chuckled. "I don't know where to start."

"Well, I've got 20 minutes before I begin teaching my next class, so tell me the highlights."

In the teachers' lounge of the international school where we worked my friend began telling me her tale. She said, "You remember the day you told me that your doors in your house were sticking?"

I remembered. The house's foundation had shifted making it impossible for the metal doors of our bedrooms to close.

She continued, "You said that you had a man from the school come and grind off the bottom a bit so they would swing freely again."

Yes, this was all true. Seemed fairly straightforward.

"Not long after, we had the same issue at our house except it was our front door. We could only open it wide enough to slide through. We called our landlord and asked if he would come fix it."

"And?"

"Well, we were waiting and waiting and he never came. Finally, he called yesterday morning to tell us that he sent his friend, Ehab, over to take care of it while we were at work. I was elated."

"So far so good," I said.

"You would think so," she said. "We returned home last night. My husband put the key in the door and pushed on it. It swung freely. We were almost ready to give kudos to our landlord when we stepped into our house. Rather than walk straight in, my husband stepped down. He turned on the light and discovered that instead of shaving the metal door so it would swing freely, Ehab had chipped out our floor tile in a perfect fan shape. All that was there now was dirt!"

I laughed. As soon as I regained my composure, I laughed some more. She joined in too and we had tears streaming down our faces.

She said her husband walked around their home the rest of the night muttering, "What in the...? Who would do such a...? I can't believe that he..."

Now they'd have to address the open floor. This pretty much sums up a lot of my cultural interactions. I expect one thing; the local person does another. Both are shocked at the other's response.

> **As soon as I regained my composure, I laughed some more.**

Culture Cue

Offer to help your other-culture friend with a home repair. Your new-to-town other-culture friend may not have all the necessary tools for the project or know where to purchase them.

15

Miriam · The "House" Next Door
Open Your Heart, Be Changed Forever

Shwyya bi shwyya ("Little by little"), we began setting up our house and getting into a routine of sorts. "Winter" (which is like summer for most parts of the Northern Hemisphere) was over and temperatures were in the triple digits in February. I would try to trick myself that it was still winter by cranking up the A/C and sitting directly underneath it while sipping hot chocolate. That is, until it quit working.

Battle stations!

We immediately called a repairman (not the well-meaning Ehab) to come and fix it as well as a leaky pipe in our bathroom. He responded quickly arriving 4 days after our request. The ironic part is that when he arrived, the electricity in the neighborhood had gone out so he could not doublecheck to see if the new part would actually correct the problem. He shrugged and said, *"Hanshoof"* ("We'll see"), and proceeded to repair the leaky pipe with a new part. We walked him out to his truck and paused to take in the view of our new neighborhood.

A variety of homes surrounded us. We shared one wall with neighbors who have a structure similar in size to ours–a three-bedroom concrete structure with more concrete and barbed wire around it serving as a fence. Across the sandy, open lot was a new construction home that is a deep red color, extremely large and modern. To the side of our house was something my mind and heart still try to process—four sticks driven into the hard ground with burlap cloth attached to them. This was the "home" for a family of at least four people from South Sudan.

I have seen poverty, but none so crushing and up-close as this. Little faces exited the structure and came to greet us as we placed some items in a storage unit. The oldest girl introduced herself as Miriam. She was 9. She pointed to her brothers telling us their names and ages (4 and 2). The boys stood side by side grinning, holding hands and wearing only worn T-shirts that almost covered their bare bottoms.

The three of them joined us in our work without any expectation. I gave them a few food items as thanks. They smiled happily and went back to their "house" to show their mother. She emerged, asking if it would be possible to fill their bucket with water. John filled it using our garden hose and returned it to grateful eyes.

John and I went inside wrecked from this experience. How do we respond? What's best? What's acceptable? What would Jesus do? My first instinct was to stay within our four walls as much as possible to avoid another scene like this. I am not sure my heart could withstand another round. I suppose such pain is good. Pain means I am not calloused to the plight of those around me. Pain drives me to prayer. Pain requires me to act.

Miriam now had a new neighbor.

Me.

Miriam crossed *my* path.

She now had an advocate.

> **Pain drives me to prayer. Pain requires me to act.**

When I set out to change the world, I did not imagine it to be this fragile, this vulnerable, this desperate. Grandiose programs, air drops, nicely tented medical clinics and classrooms...that was my idea of serving a group of people. Until Miriam.

But Miriam served *me* even when she needed food, clothes and a secure place to sleep. How does *that* fit in my plan? I am not sure it does, but it does fit within the character of Jesus to look Miriam in the eyes and really see her, her potential and her need.

As I thought about this, I heard the drip, drip, dripping sound coming from a leaky hose in our bathroom. The newly replaced part had sprung a leak. That morning I had been thoroughly annoyed by this inconvenience. After Miriam, I am thankful for a wonderful place to live.

However, this isn't the end.

I do not live my life without hope.

I do not want Miriam to either.

Our connection can bring deeper conversations and forged opportunities.

I want to look away, but Jesus compels me to enter the fray.

Am I willing?

Culture Cue

Be sensitive of your other-culture friend's history. She may have left her country under difficult circumstances. Allow her to tell her story.

16

Hayah · Hen(na) Party
Live Inclusively, Create Community

I've never been one for body decorating, but I received an invitation from a parent at the school to come for a henna party. I did not say "Hen Party" though John would probably disagree.

Emileigh and Aria encouraged me to accept. I seriously had to think long and hard about this. On the one hand, I wanted to experience this truly Sudanese cultural tradition. Henna is a plant-based dye used to decorate a woman's arms and legs; however, I doubt the FDA of Sudan had any regulations or standards regarding its use. On the other hand, I knew that the henna once applied would be temporary but 2 to 3 months temporary.

I have seven layers of skin. Let's do this.

On the day of the party, the girls and I met up with seven other friends who had also been invited. We arrived a little after 6 p.m. and were welcomed at the gate of a beautiful home. To the right of the gate was an enclosed courtyard full of blossoming trees and vivid green grass. We stared at it. Green anything is something to be savored here.

Hayah (the host mother) greeted us warmly with a handshake and a kiss on each cheek. She was happy to meet Aria and Emileigh's *om* (mother). She motioned for us to enter her home. We sat on large, ornate couches. I soaked in the scene of an imposing marble staircase and the lavish gold-colored decor.

We visited for a few minutes, before she directed us to another room. This room had two large beds and a couch. She turned on the air conditioning and said, "This will be better." I agree.

Hayah left the room and we chatted among ourselves until one of the house help came to serve us fruit juice in beautiful goblets. We toasted to the goodness of the Lord and sipped.

Next, a basket of chocolates was passed around. I am not sure about much in this culture, but it cannot be bad if the dinner starts with chocolate. Yet another basket was passed which held small homemade cookies covered in powdered sugar. This lady was batting a thousand.

A dark-complected woman with a headwrap introduced herself. She pulled out her tools and we realized she was the "Henna Lady" (HL). She showed us designs on her cellphone (I thought that was very sophisticated technology) and asked which ones we would like.

I am learning that in this society "less is boring and more is best."

I sat and watched for a bit before it became my turn. HL began drawing on each lady's arm or styling freehand as she went. I could not decide which pattern to choose. I finally turned her loose and said, "Be free. Draw whatever you would like."

She chose a floral pattern. The ink was thicker than I expected. It looked more like black gel icing than ink. After she drew the design, we had to sit carefully so as not to disturb the artwork. I was a frozen mannequin. My biggest fear was forgetting about the ink and scratching my nose or wiping my face.

As each woman was "henna'd" our hostess would pass out plates of food. Crescent rolls with cheese filling, mini-pizzas, a small calzone and cornbread rounded out this entrée. I carefully ate keeping in mind the wet ink.

I only had her do one hand at first. Then the girls told me that married women can have two hands done and even their feet. HL made her rounds until everyone was sitting carefully and nibbling as best they could. HL started to stand up but we motioned her back and had her start Round 2 of inking. She did not seem too annoyed with us.

When she came to me, I decided on a small area on my left hand that would be designed around my wedding ring. She added a bit more flourish than I would have liked, but I am learning that in this society "less is boring and more is best."

Some girls told me that many Sudanese women have henna designs done right before their wedding as a way to be beautiful for their husbands. Others (like our hostess) have a new henna design drawn every couple months.

Emileigh loved her design. She told me she was "hooked" and could not wait to have more designs done at a later date. Aria was already planning her next idea.

The ink on my hands was beginning to dry. I wondered what would happen next. We continued to sit, chat and snack. I spoke a bit of Arabic with Hayah and she laughed at my Egyptian accent. I assured her I was doing my best to develop a Sudanese accent, but she patted my shoulder and told me, "No problem."

I found out that this Muslim lady had three young children and was also studying medicine at the local university. Impressive by any standard.

After about 2 hours of ink drying, Hayah told us it was time to wash our henna. We all paraded into the bathrooms and began rinsing the excess dye off of our hands. Miraculously, the design stayed even with a scrubbing of soap. We dried off and Hayah handed us lotion to rub over the design to preserve it until it completely set.

The evening was winding down and we asked Hayah if we could do a group picture. She agreed and we posed together. She kissed our cheeks again and walked us to our vehicles, waving as we drove away.

I was thankful for the experience, thankful for the relationships that the international school provided and thankful for Hayah who included me in part of her Sudanese life.

I could begin to see my life unfolding here albeit ink-stained.

Culture Cue

Throw a birthday party or a baby shower for your other-culture friend. Many cultures have seen Western celebrations on TV and long to be a part of one. Check any special dietary restrictions they may have ahead of time.

17

Mr. Habib · The Home Visit
Ask Questions, People's Stories Reveal

Though it may have reverberated like the beat of a one-armed drummer, we developed into a bit of a rhythm in Khartoum. I still have to shake myself a bit when I type that. Seriously? Khartoum? Pam lived in Khartoum? Sounds like a bad sitcom. Most of the time it felt like it could be.

A Sudanese co-worker at the school, Nala, invited us to her home for dinner. The directions we received from her father were: "Turn at orange container, go down dirt road, look for cream house." Khartoum is home to 8 million people and approximately three street signs. Finding anything proved challenging.

We had his phone number. As we neared the vicinity of their home, John called. Mr. Habib walked outside and began waving his arms. We had arrived. They asked us to come at 6 p.m. so we arrived a few minutes after (as is proper here).

John tapped our host's right shoulder in a traditional Sudanese greeting. I smiled nervously and presented the official "Let's Be Friends Dessert," lemon poppyseed pound cake.

Mr. Habib accepted the cake and ushered us into the living room which was painted in a soothing pale yellow. The furnishings were beautifully arranged, simple and comfortable.

A man in his 50s, Mr. Habib was a successful electrical engineer who spoke brilliant English. I was relieved after our 11-hour home visit in Egypt with an Arabic/English dictionary between us.

We began small talk. All of the women (myself included) left our headwraps on in this Muslim home to show respect to this family who had welcomed us so kindly.

Nala left for a few minutes returning with glasses of fresh mango juice on a silver tray. We each sipped and asked about their family, home and neighborhood. I told Nala that the girls loved to shop at the local markets. Her eyes brightened and said, "Really? There's one right behind us!"

She jumped up and invited the girls to join her in a market tour. "Just to look," she said. While they were away, we spoke with Mr. Habib who told us he was Nubian. John asked him about his town where he grew up. Mr. Habib said he lived in an area that was permanently flooded by a dam that had been built near his home. He and his entire family had to leave the place where Nubians had lived for thousands of years.

Such a sad story, but he opened his heart and shared his pain.

He pulled out a book and showed us maps of the villages before the dam was built and after. Such a sad story, but he opened his heart and shared his pain. We were grateful. I breathed a prayer that Jesus would be near him and bless this family.

He told us of his travels and how he had learned Arabic, English and French since his initial Nubian language upbringing. We were impressed. Four languages. I am still inserting ninth grade Spanish into my Arabic conjugations.

The girls returned after an hour and stayed in the courtyard to visit with the rest of the family. We met Mr. Habib's wife and his other sons and daughters. Near us a small grill of heated coals held a selection of lamb pieces that smelled amazing.

Around 8:30 p.m., we were invited into the dining area. A lovely table was set for us plus Mr. Habib and Nala. The other family members gathered at another table in another room. The food was delicious (and not just because it was way past my normal dinner time).

We commented many times "*Akl lazeez*" ("The food is very delicious"). After several helpings (thanks to our host's prodding), we leaned back in our chairs and indicated that our "tanks" were very full.

Mr. Habib invited us to join him in the courtyard. We relaxed a bit before Nala brought us dessert. She scooped large portions of vanilla pudding that contained bits of cookies and fruit. Again, very good, but painful.

From our study of Sudanese culture, we understood that before a visit ends we would be offered one last cup of tea. To leave sooner than that would be considered extremely rude. So we talked with different family members for the next hour waiting for the tea to arrive. We waited and talked.

Finally around 10 p.m., John thanked Mr. Habib for a lovely evening. Then we sat some more. Still no tea. John realized at this point that probably no tea was coming, so he stood up to begin the exiting process. An international incident would have to be risked.

We followed his lead, began shaking hands and thanking each family member for a beautiful evening. They walked us to our vehicle where we climbed in and waved as we drove away.

We arrived home around 11 p.m., tired but thankful for the opportunity to connect with this sweet family. So no "farewell tea." Well, chalk up one for culture abhorrations. I guess there is no formula for living life with people. Let's call it "organic."

Culture Cue

Help an other-culture person understand by explaining what you mean through non-verbal gestures.

18

Priya · Hot, Spicy English Club
Realize Differences, Discover Similarities

My face turned red as I tried to keep a smile.

"You like?" Priya asked.

I nodded.

"I made it just for you, Teacher!"

I smiled again and tried to casually pick up my water bottle to take a sip. Regaining my composure I said, "Wow, Priya! That is really spicy!"

She laughed and said, "Oh no, Teacher! I put little spice in food for you. Not big spice."

I laughed and said, "I think big spice."

Priya pulled out two more plastic containers and set them in front of me. "You must also try these!"

The ladies around me waited for my response. I took the spoon, prayed "Lord, impress someone in America to send me Nexium" and scooped bites out of each dish.

"You like?"

"I do like it, Priya. Very much."

She leaned back satisfied. I turned to the other women and said, "I don't like to eat alone. Join me."

As we enjoyed a meal together, I looked at this diverse group of women: 1 Indian Hindu, 1 Korean Christian, 3 Egyptian Muslims,

1 Egyptian Christian and 1 American Christian. Together we made up The Parents' English Club which was held at the school where I worked.

I met with these ladies several times a week to discuss life with the hopes of improving their English. Of course, as a teacher I had lesson plans and objectives. They just came wrapped with casual topics, spontaneous laughter and food...lots of food.

Because of our diverse backgrounds, we spent a good deal of our time sharing traditions, customs and recipes. Priya got the ball rolling with her dishes of Spicy, More Spicy and Melt Your Face.

Others soon joined and we brought dishes at least once a week for everyone to try. I brought various items, but the group's favorites were lasagne and Texas sheet cake. In the best accented English she could muster, one Egyptian lady said, "Teacher, I love your Texas sh*t cake too, too much!"

I thanked her. Then I said, "You know. That's a long name for a cake. Let's just call it Texas cake from now on." She shrugged and agreed.

Each club day, the women would trickle in, chatting with one another before we started. On the table I kept a book entitled *1,000 Questions*. At the beginning of the session, I would ask one woman to choose a question from the book and we would all have to answer to the best of our ability in English and we had to answer truthfully. Everyone agreed.

At times, these questions would be met with a period of silence as each would reflect on her beliefs.

As they were getting to know each other, the questions at the beginning of the book were chosen. Questions such as, "What's your favorite movie?" or "Where did you grow up?"

As the weeks passed, I noticed that the questions were moving into deeper inquiries such as, "What is truth?" "What happens when you die?" "Do good people go to heaven?"

At times, these questions would be met with a period of silence as each would reflect on her beliefs.

One Muslim woman said, "I don't know if I go to Paradise. Only Allah knows."

Priya said, "We have many gods. Actions decide your fate."

The Korean Christian answered, "I have peace that Jesus is waiting for me in heaven."

I sensed a heavenly moment. I could sense the presence of the Lord thickly. How He loved these women, these beautiful, sincere, open creations of His.

Someone said something in that moment that shifted the mood. They began chasing another topic. I did not mind. Truth is revealed most often in increments.

Toward the end of the semester, the ladies wanted to plan a holiday buffet. One Egyptian lady brought a beef and noodle dish, but shook her finger at Priya the Hindu, and said, "You no eat. Cow!"

Then the Korean lady pointed at her pot stickers and said to the Muslims, "You no eat. Pork!"

Priya smiled broadly and pointed at her dish. She said, "We *all* eat. Vegetables!"

Everyone laughed and then asked her if they were *spicy* vegetables.

She said, "Of course! I am Indian!"

We talked about everything in our hearts all while asking questions, gaining understanding and giving respect. We loved each other and took time to really listen.

And even some English vocabulary grew.

Priya grew to be a good friend of mine. With tearful goodbyes we parted as she and her family moved to join her husband in his new job location.

As we embraced one another through watery eyes, she said, "You must make it spicy!"

Yes, indeed, Priya. Life is no good when it is bland and full of sameness. May I always keep it spicy with rich friendships from all walks of life and dairy nearby to wash it down.

Culture Cue

Invite your other-culture friend over for a dinner or party to introduce him to other people. Stay near your other-culture friend throughout the event to help him navigate the social setting.

19

Abdel · The Pakistani General
Cross Social Strata, Find Unique Opportunities

As we were in our ninth month of life in Sudan, the drop in temperature to a mere 105 degrees had me reaching for my jacket and a cup of hot apple cider. Okay, maybe not. However, the calendar indicated autumn had come so I decorated the house with scattered pumpkins, fall leaves and a sporadic pilgrim here and there. A scented candle wafting through the house had actually convinced me for a few solitary moments the seasons were indeed changing.

A friend further along in the journey told me that, even if the weather does not change in your location, decorate your house as if it does to help it feel like time and seasons are passing. So I did. It does at least while I am inside.

Outside our home our Muslim friends celebrated a significant holiday—*Eid al Fitr* or "Festival of Conclusion of the Fast." They had much cause to celebrate because this *eid* celebrated the conclusion of the 30 days of dawn-to-sunset fasting (including water) during the entire month of Ramadan. Ramadan fasting is one of five pillars in Islam.

- *Shahadah*: sincerely reciting the Muslim profession of faith
- *Salat*: performing ritual prayers in the proper way five times each day

- *Zakat*: paying an alms (or charity) tax to benefit the poor and the needy
- *Sawm*: fasting during the month of Ramadan
- *Hajj*: pilgrimage to Mecca

A faithful Muslim will practice all five throughout his life with the hopes that Allah will see that the scale of good works is tipped in the believer's favor allowing him into paradise. But the follower can never know for sure of Allah's judgment while in this life, leaving him determined to prove his faithfulness.

> **This life costs, but it also rewards.**

Once Ramadan concludes, there is a collective societal sigh of relief and *Eid al Fitr* begins.

This particular *eid*, John and I along with some other teachers were invited into the home of one of our students. This family recently arrived from Pakistan and was anxious to make friends. The mother, Noor, greeted us warmly and directed us to sit in their family room (sometimes called a "*saloon*" or "*salon*" depending on your accent). Noor then brought us fruit juice to drink as she prepared our tea.

We spoke with the three children ranging in ages from 4 to 11, asking about their hobbies and their favorite subjects. The children spoke Urdu which is a Pakistani language, attended an English-speaking school and were also learning Arabic because of their current context. I, as a youngster, watched Bugs Bunny on Saturdays.

The father, Abdel, invited us to the dinner table where a variety of steaming, colorful dishes were prepared. I thought we were having tea and we were, but tea also included chicken, sandwiches, *samosas* (little triangle pastries with veggie fillings), fried potatoes, salad and a sweet pudding. I wondered what a dinner with them would look like.

A high ranking official in his country's army, Abdel told us he had been stationed in Khartoum to do training with the Sudanese military. He included that this is his family's first time living abroad.

"Me, too!" I exclaimed.

71

Noor and I had an immediate connection. We would learn this country together.

Noor continued to pour cups of tea and offer bowls of candy as the children proudly showed us their latest dance moves. John and Abdel spoke together as fathers, each smiling broadly as they recounted their children's feats.

Soon our time came to a close but only after Abdel and Noor invited us to return for an authentic Pakistani dinner. Abdel promised he would not make the food too spicy since he knows we cannot take it. We did not contradict him.

We thanked them profusely, said our goodbyes and walked to our vehicle with the entire family following. Abdel invited all of us to "stop by anytime" and shook our hands once more.

John and I drove away once again shaking our heads. Did we just have dinner with a Pakistani general? Did this loud-mouthed, blonde-headed, blue-eyed Christian American woman sit with this family and dine without incident?

The ever-infamous plane ticket that took me from a place of deep relationships also brought beautiful opportunities to share life with people I would have never known any other way. This life costs, but it also rewards.

Our friends that day were proof of that. Borders are not just geographic lines. They exist in our hearts and our psyches as well. When we cross them, we are introduced to a whole new world. That day I was so grateful to have stepped over the line.

Culture Cue

It is difficult to be in another country without extended family. Offer to watch your other-culture friend's children for a while so she can go out. This, of course, is after you have had several interactions and built trust.

20

The Uncle · The Dance of Negotiations
Learn to Negotiate, Don't Take It Personally

My computer had 9:58 p.m. as the time when our guests finally exited our home with John accompanying them to the gate. He walked into a side room where I had been waiting and sighed a deep sigh, "Whew. It's over. We don't have to move."

It all started in January when we first arrived in Khartoum. We were unbelievably happy to discover that a home would be available for us to move into immediately upon arrival. That is not typical. Normally, those arriving would spend a few days (unfortunately sometimes weeks) looking for a decent place and reasonable rent. Two conditions that do not always coincide.

Once we had settled in nicely, we waited for our landlord to come by and greet us. No one came. John reviewed the contract from our friends who were the previous renters and realized that the agreement continued for another 5 months. Still, we were not the ones who signed the contract, so we thought someone would eventually show up. Wrong. We lived in the house past the date of the contract with no discussion of a new agreement.

We needed to leave the city so we left some emergency numbers with several people in case the landlord showed up and wanted additional payment. Once we were gone, the landlord did show up and asked to speak to us. Our friend told him that we would return in 3 weeks and could speak to us then.

We returned and played phone tag a few more times still not settling on any specific meeting date. I could not figure out how this was all supposed to work. We continued the dance.

Finally, we received a call from an uncle in the landlord's family requesting we meet together. Great! Let's get this thing done! An uncle, the landlady and one more man (whom we were unsure of his role) arrived in the early evening 8 months after we had moved in. I offered them glasses of cold water and was heating tea water for later.

John and I greeted them in Arabic. We soon discovered that at least two of them spoke English. We asked each other about their health, families, weather and then asked about it again and a third time. (That is proper Sudanese custom.) Eventually, the rent discussions came. Their request: we pay them what was listed in the previous contract in U.S. dollars that evening for rent past and for rent extending through the next year.

John graciously thanked them for their request and then spoke with them about a water leak we had in one bathroom. He showed them that water was coming through the concrete walls and the outlets. (John told me this was a bad thing.) They nodded their heads in agreement and said it should be fixed. We all paused and waited.

The uncle said we could have it fixed and deduct it from the rent. We countered that the leaking wall in question was a structural wall, and we did not want to be the ones taking a hammer to it. They agreed they would send someone to fix it. They also looked at a structural beam that had suffered a bit of damage during an earthquake tremor in the summer. That would also be fixed, they assured us.

John told them that once the house was repaired we would gladly re-enter into negotiations. They asked once more if we did not want to just go ahead and pay since the landlady was leaving the country soon. We thanked them, but told them we would rather wait. They left soon after for another appointment. The dance continued.

A few days later we received a call telling us that the plumber would be coming to our house on Monday at 1 p.m. To work on the wall. We told them we would be waiting. No plumber came. Not Monday. Not Tuesday. Not any day that week.

A trip to East Sudan had been planned for the weekend. We were now on the return leg of the travel when we received a call from the plumber. He was sitting outside our house ready to work. Six days later. We regretfully told him we were not at the house. He was disappointed.

Four days later, we received another call that the plumber would be at our house at 1 p.m. We hurried through our office work at the school and made it back just in time...to wait. We waited until 5:30 p.m. That night and wondered if somehow the cable companies in America were the ones who scheduled the Sudanese plumbers. He did eventually arrive and worked from 5:30 to 8 p.m. including two trips with John to the hardware store to purchase parts.

The bathroom was now finished and leak-free. It took 9 months, but the moment had arrived. John and I thought about a grand opening event complete with ribbon cutting and punch, but our celebratory plans were cut short when we saw a new drip forming by the sink. Twenty-three hours we had Plumbing Nirvana. Now it was over. Sigh.

The voices continued back and forth in a verbal volley...

This story is long, but so were the negotiations. We did not hear from the landlady or uncle. The next call came from the landlady's son who lived in Qatar. At 10:15 p.m. he began more negotiations with John. John had been in bed and had dozed when the call came. Smart tactics for the other side. He and John spoke back and forth for over an hour debating the cost of rent, length of stay and home improvement purchases. No resolution was found.

The following day when we were in a meeting, John received another call. The uncle asked if we could meet again. John agreed that we would meet at 7:30 p.m. Around 8:20 p.m., the uncle and another man (a different unknown) arrived. I stepped into a side room and began praying since no women were present to host, and I shouldn't remain in the room.

Over glasses of water, I listened to their voices rise and fall for 90 minutes. At times, laughter would erupt and I thought they came to an agreement. Then at other times, the uncle would seem to be shouting his point. John stepped into the side room to get some cash from the safe. He looked me in the eye and asked, "So are you ready to move this weekend if we have to?" I told him I would do whatever we had to do.

He disappeared again and presented the family with 3 previous months' rent in cash. Now the negotiations would be for the coming months. John told the man he did not want to keep the former contract. He wanted to create a new one. The uncle wondered why we just would not hand over the cash, but knew he must continue or lose a renter.

The voices continued back and forth in a verbal volley until glasses were refilled and their energy regained momentum. At last John walked into our room and retrieved a stack of cash from our safe. He counted it out in front of me and smiled. We had reached agreement.

John laid the money on the table. They counted the money which would cover the next 9 months of rent. John asked them if they were happy with the settlement. The uncle assured John they were and that anything he said in passion was because he was representing his sister's interest. Then he smiled and said, "We friends, yes?"

I laughed as I overheard his question. John, as an academic dean, had experienced on a number of occasions parents who were, shall we say, "passionate" about their child's academic career. He had seen flapping arms, heard raised voices and negotiated terms with entire families. Most always after an agreement had been reached, they would laugh and pat him on the back while extending an invitation to dinner. They were not permanently angry, just in persuasive mode.

The uncle waited for John's response.

John said, "Yes, yes. We are friends." He then asked for a receipt for all the cash exchanged and shook the men's hands. He walked them out, returning thoroughly exhausted from the evening's transactions.

He told me, "You can now settle in. We're good through next year. Then the dance starts all over again."

Culture Cue

Give your other-culture friend permission to ask questions. He is curious about so many things he may see, but may think it rude to ask unless given permission.

21

Abdelrahman · Goat Parts, Part 2
Place Yourself With People, Gather Insight

A cousin of a cousin invited John and me along with some other friends to leave the city limits of Khartoum and traverse across the desert to a remote village of Bedouins. Anxious to "get out of Dodge" we loaded a Land Rover and headed out.

Mile after mile, sand stretched as far as the eye could see.

"I don't suppose AAA services reach this far, huh?" I muttered.

There are few major roads making it difficult to get lost, but still I felt like we had left earth and were now exploring the terrain of the moon. The desert does have its own beauty; what it does not have is a 7-11.

We drove for hours until we came upon a village that appeared like a mirage. When we got out, the buildings had not vanished under the heat of the sun. We were grateful to have arrived.

The homes were different than those in Khartoum. While there were some typical square concrete homes, there were also thatched domiciles with rounded roofs. The rounded ceilings served well to deflect the sun's direct rays and also allowed the heat to capture inside at the top of the room leaving the bottom area cooler.

We were greeted by a young man in his early teens who directed us into a nicely painted concrete home. He pointed and motioned for us to sit on the plastic covered couches that lined the perimeter of the walls.

We were a bit nervous and did not want to do anything to offend. Soon a man with a white *jalibaya* (robe) and *tageya* (traditional hat) sporting a full black beard walked toward us. The men rose to greet him as he introduced himself.

"I am Abdelrahman, *sheikh* (respected leader) of this village," he said, proudly.

The women in our group remained silent as the men introduced each of us.

Abdelrahman sat down on the straw mat on the floor in front of the couches and directed us to join him. He began asking questions, "How long did it take you to get here? What do you think of Sudan? Is it hot like this in America?"

The men directed the conversation. Frankly, I was relieved. All that was popping into my head at that moment was, "So do camels really spit?" or "Is Omar Sharif a friend of yours?" Yeah, better to remain quiet.

The young man returned with a silver tray with bottles of cold water on it. We were grateful to wash the dust down.

When the conversation would lull, we would just listen to the sounds of the village, children laughing and goats braying. Different, but comfortable.

Abdelrahman jumped from his place and said, "Come. We meet my family." With brisk steps, he took us into another building this one bigger and colorfully painted.

"This is my house," he said. "The other is my mother's."

We nodded.

"Come! Come!" he said as he took us room to room.

As we rounded the corner to the kitchen, a woman in a veil holding a small baby was working.

"This is my wife, but if you are lucky you will be wife #2," he said to one of our accompanying females.

She ignored the remark and commented to the woman that her baby was beautiful. The woman's eyes lit up. What mother does not like to hear that?

The women chatted with her for a bit before Abdelrahman said, "Come! Come!"

He told us about his family's history. They were nomadic. His father and grandfather were camel herders who moved across Sudan's deserts in search of grass for their animals. When the camels were ready for market, they would gather at this village to prepare for the journey to sell them.

Abdelrahman said that many Bedouins still live in tents and wander the deserts, but he has a permanent structure. He now hires camel herders so he can stay home.

We returned to the room with the mat and couches, sitting once again as glasses of fresh-squeezed juices were offered. We sipped as he told us more about his life and Islam.

"You know," he said smiling, "in Islam you can have four wives."

John answered, "I find that one is plenty."

They both laughed and I was not sure whether to be proud or give him the look. The conversation was interrupted when the young man appeared yet again with a very large silver tray. He struggled to reach the handles on either side.

He placed the tray in the middle of the circle and left.

Abdelrahman said, "Ah! It's ready. You are my guests. Eat! Eat!"

I looked at the tray. On a bed of browned rice lay a perfectly shaped roasted goat who had been curled into a circle to fit the shape of the tray. When I say "perfectly-shaped" that is to say he had feet, head, eyes and a tongue whose last words were probably, "I should have listened to my mother."

Some in our group had experienced a similar type of meal. I had not and was mesmerized. I am not used to all the parts being connected and in the shape of something recognizable. I prefer my meat the way God intended, cut up, sanitized and on a Styrofoam plastic tray in the freezer section. This was so...free-range.

The *sheikh* encouraged everyone to take a handful of meat and begin eating. I promptly put my left hand under my leg so as not to be tempted to use it. (It is considered unclean.) I watched my friends take pieces of meat and bits of rice and scoop it into their mouths.

I pulled a small piece and grabbed some rice and promptly lost all of it somewhere in my head scarf. Snap. I tried again.

Abdelrahman clicked his tongue. "You all do not know how to eat meat. Let me show you." He then licked each finger on his right hand, plunged it into the goat's midriff and pulled out a large chunk of meat. Smiling he pushed it straight toward me and said, "This is how you eat meat."

I thanked him and took the meat while pondering the word *vegetarian* in Arabic.

Everyone continued trying to do their best to get the food from the tray to their mouths. A ring of rice around us said we were not that successful.

Abdelrahaman grinned and said, "Now for this!" He took his thumb and placed it

How did it come to this? How did I get here?

in the socket of the goat's eye and flicked the eyeball out. As he held it in his hand, the eye looked at me and inquired, "Did we ever think we'd come to this?"

"Never in a million years, Goat Eyeball," I answered. I was having an out-of-body experience.

Who does this?

Where am I?

Not less than two years ago, I went to malls, saw movies and ate unseeing things with forks.

How did it come to this?

How did I get here?

Before I could check to see if my United Airlines app would work, Abdelrahman pushed the eyeball toward me and said, "This is for very special guests. The oldest guest."

It was my turn to smile. "I'm not the oldest. John's older than me." Sorry, husband, it is survival of the fittest out here.

He smiled and said, "I'm not the oldest either. My friend here is."

Our friend had no where to go. He was in truth the oldest and also the classiest because he said, "Thank you very much, Sheik. This is an honor." And he popped that eyeball in his mouth and swallowed it down.

Things can only get better from here I surmised. And it did.

The young man returned this time with a huge collection of fresh fruit. I breathed a sigh of relief.

"Bananas, how I love you!" I whispered.

Abdelrahman offered a pitcher of water following the meal for us to wash our hands. We all leaned back, complimenting the meal multiple times. Serving goat for most Sudanese is reserved for special occasions. We had been honored by this act and we were grateful.

Tea was served and we sipped the steaming, sticky sweet tea in comfortable silence. As we placed the empty tea cups on the tray, the men began the process of departing. They thanked our host again for his kindness, the tour, the history and the beautiful meal. We then sat a bit longer and it started again.

At the third thank you, the men stood and the women followed suit. Abdelrahman was satisfied with this though he did the traditionally correct response, saying, "No, you must stay here with me tonight and forever."

He walked us to the vehicle and said that we were welcome in his home and village any time. He waved goodbye as we began our return trek to Khartoum.

He is also a Sudanese brother who loves Jesus, a brilliant businessman and a fiercely loyal friend...

I smiled.

Who does stuff like this?

Who eats goat parts on a mat with friends hosted by a Bedouin *sheikh*?

Who meets amazing people loved by God out in the middle of a desert?

I do and I could not be more thankful.

Culture Cue

In many cultures saying no to a request is considered rude. Your other-culture friend may agree to visit or attend an event with you, but actually not mean it. Ask your friend how she would decline an invitation in her culture. This will help you understand her answer to your invitations. "Yes" may not mean "yes" and "no" may not mean "no" the first or second time.

22

The Advocate · Pam's First Wreck
Be Open, Find a True Friend

Fisher-Price makes a variety of toys to commemorate the "firsts" of children. Toys like "My First Purse," "My First Bike," and the new "My First Debit Card." They may, however, want to dip into the Sudanese market for new, global-friendly ideas.

If they were to produce a new city scene called, "My First Wreck," they would need a truck, a van known as an *ahmjaht*, a *tok-tok* (3-wheeled passenger vehicle), another van, another *tok-tok*, random passersby, drivers, translators, a man selling socks and the skinniest police officer ever seen.

My day had started out a little iffy. I had finished teaching art class with three groups of preschoolers and I was going home to wash off all of the "creative energy" they had bestowed on my clothes through the medium of paint.

I called John from the house and asked him if he wanted me to bring lunch to him at the school. He agreed, so I began driving from the south side of town to the north side. John had just shown me a handy-dandy shortcut a couple days before, so I decided to be adventurous and try it all by myself. (Foreshadowing...)

Traffic in Khartoum is nothing short of a video game. At any time vans, taxis, buses, donkey carts, and *tok-toks* can come flying at you from any side. Conventional road rules do not apply. If there is a shorter way to get there, they will take it regardless of the current flow of traffic.

I had almost reached my destination at a little restaurant called "Coffee World." I had planned to stop in and get sandwiches for John and me. I had just turned on my blinker and was proceeding to make a left turn when pow! bang! crash. A blue *ahmjaht* sideswiped me from the back left of our truck to the now-inverted side mirror.

The driver looked through his window and began yelling at me. Yes, you read that right. He veered to the left of my truck turning left and he yells at me. Of course, my Arabic training does not include curses, so I am thankfully understanding very little of what he is saying.

I promptly called John relaying to him the situation. He immediately tried to call our friend who was our "get-us-out-of-every-possible-Arabic-speaking-trouble-situation-possible" guy. He is also a Sudanese brother who loves Jesus, a brilliant businessman and a fiercely loyal friend. I will call him from now on "The Advocate." Unfortunately, our Advocate was off-site and would be delayed a bit.

I tried to keep it together, praying and chastising myself for not having eyes in the back of my head. Drivers trying to get around the accident were yelling, shouting, honking and pointing.

The *ahmjaht* driver was trying to convince me to just drive away. His vehicle was fine. Our truck, however, was not. I told him in my best Arabic that this was a big problem and he should not go anywhere. Then I pulled out a very official scrap of paper and wrote down his license plate number just to show him I was serious. It must have worked because he pulled off to the side and parked.

Curious, a *tok-tok* driver stopped to see what was happening to the foreigner who had a dazed look on her face. He asked Mr. Ahmjat what had happened. Soon another van driver stopped; walkers decided to get in on it, too. At least 50 men were now surrounding Mr. Ahmjat and me.

John arrived at the scene a few minutes later. I had never been so relieved in my life. He asked one of the men in the crowd if the police had been called. The man shrugged and patted John saying, "Issokay. Issokay."

One man who could speak a bit of English and Arabic agreed to translate between the two groups, Team Pam and Team Amjaht. The translator yelled key points in English to us and Arabic to the others while also inserting his opinion. Soon words and arms were flying like an old Bruce Lee movie. I stayed quietly in the truck hoping somehow to be beamed somewhere, anywhere.

John realized that an important registration paper for the truck was not in the glove compartment. The police would require it so he had to go to the house to get it. I did not want to be left "alone," but our Advocate arrived and assured John he would stay with me. John thanked him, patted my hand and left.

The next 30 minutes or so were spent in varied conversations with random people none of whom had been present at the accident, but who all had firm opinions about the situation. Our Advocate kept most of the others at bay, while I sat in the truck with the door open.

One man, thinking he would seize the moment, gave me opportunity to buy a quantity of men's socks in a variety of colors. When I told him, "No thanks," he continued until I gave him a look that must have communicated, "Perhaps today is not a good day for stocking sales." He shuffled away and began working the rest of the crowd.

Finally, a police officer (size 20-inch waist) arrived in his white uniform and blue cap. He asked that we all proceed to the police station.

At the station I first had my name registered in a very large book where one of the officers handwrote "Bam Morteen Zheene." It was supposed to be "Pamela Jeane Morton," but I understand because I struggle spelling Sudanese names.

I was then directed to another office (of sorts...3 walls) where desks were set up in a U-shape and officers lined the perimeter. Various citizens were sitting in the provided chairs using colorful, boisterous ways to make their point. I sat in a squeaking, wooden chair and kept my eyes low. (It is considered flirtatious to look men in the eyes in this culture.)

Soon an older distinguished-looking officer began taking statements from Mr. Ahmjaht and me. I stated my case once and went silent. Mr. Amjaht, however, saw this as an opportunity to get in his two cents, three nickels, and five quarters. He began adding some details that were not true. The Advocate patiently and kindly disagreed with the man's account. He then retold my version of the story. Thankfully, the officer listened.

The police officer leaned back, made a clicking noise with his tongue, told the driver that he was clearly wrong and should stop arguing. This just made the driver argue all the more. The increased volume got the interest of two other officers who joined in the discussion.

I had never found the floor so fascinating before or prayer so easy. I just let the volume ebb and flow until I had been addressed again for more information.

The officer used my driver's license and Mr. Amjaht's to demonstrate what happened with our cars sliding them on the desk in a re-creation that a CSI guy might appreciate. Once he was satisfied with the story, he pulled out his ruler, an ink pen and a piece of paper. He began to draw the scene asking questions as he progressed. He showed me his work and asked me to sign my name agreeing that this is what occurred. He then asked the same of the driver who was still not happy but resigned himself to the outcome.

Our papers were copied and registered into the police report. Finally, our Advocate smiled and told us we were finished for the day.

I had not gone to prison.

I was free.

We would have to come back the next day for the official police report which would then need to be taken to the insurance company of the other driver. The police officer looked at me and said, "I am so sorry that this process took so long." I could have hugged him, but refrained. We left the police station and I promise you the sky was bluer, the air fresher, the honks louder. Life was good and scary, but mostly good.

As John and I drove away I told him, "There is no possible appropriate thank you gift that we can give our Advocate after a day like today."

He agreed. Our friend put himself in the middle of the fray (our fray) and willingly became our Advocate. So like Jesus. So very thankful for our Sudanese friend.

Culture Cue

Ask yourself if you have any cultural biases about your other-culture neighbor. Do these biases keep you from forming a friendship with him?

23

Village People · Going North
Give Much, Receive Much More

Five men in white *jalibayas* and turbans stood shoulder to shoulder facing us as we began our approach to a remote desert village 300 km north of Khartoum. Flanked by two pick-up trucks, they looked imposing. I felt the last ounce of bravery drain away. I had seen too many action flicks. Nothing good ever came of this scenario. Our truck with our driver continued advancing. I did not even have one of those ear pieces to call for back up.

The men began waving their arms. I looked at Aria, then John. They were wondering what to make of this, too. I prayed silently and waited. No turning back now.

Our driver pulled up to the entrance of the village, turned off the engine and signaled for John to get out.

911? AAA? Jack Bauer? Why did I not think this through?! I almost came unraveled at the potential danger of this situation when I shook myself and prayed. I did not pray, "Get me outta here!" but rather "Lord, help us demonstrate Your love, come what may."

Calm and peace prevailed. I watched as John gave the traditional Sudanese greeting and talked with each man. Afterward, they all walked toward the truck and were bustling to pull our luggage from the back. One man directed us toward our new domicile where we would be staying for the week. The sign above the door read in Arabic, "The Manager." We were going to be staying in the Principal's office.

Aria and I smiled at each other as they put plastic chairs in a corner of the room and directed us to sit. We thanked them and watched as these kind people made sure everything in our room was ready for us.

It started when John assumed the role of academic dean at an international school in Khartoum. At the beginning of each school year, teachers arrived a few days early for room preparation, training and orientation.

John managed the curriculum and professional development for the teaching staff. Prior to this, he spent the summer writing a manual of various teacher training concepts to use during the school's orientation time. After the week-long orientation, word had reached the Education Department in Sudan regarding the training.

A representative from their department asked if John would offer this same training to 40 teachers in Khartoum. He agreed. This was an amazing opportunity. Soon after, the Undersecretary of Education asked if John would be willing to do this same work-shop in his home village in northern Sudan. He assured us that the Department of Education would cover all expenses related to the event. What? Wow!

After a few attempts at coordinating schedules with the village elders, we found mutual dates that would work. John gathered his materials—whiteboard, easel, computer, projector, surge protector, etc. I gathered toilet paper, hand sanitizer, bug spray, mosquito netting, clean sheets and peanut butter. Aria charged her iPod, packed gummies and mangos. We were ready.

As Aria and I sat in the chairs in this principal's office, we noticed they had just recently installed a new air cooler. It was not working yet so one of the men rolled in a portable one and turned it on full blast 4 feet away from us. Again, we were moved by their thoughtfulness. Next, they needed to do work inside the office so they carried our chairs over to a small porch area and signaled for us to sit. John joined us. They brought us chilled bottles of water and they banged and yelled and coerced the cooler into working. They exited the doorway with big smiles. Success.

One man told John that the village had electricity, but was not on the national grid. This meant there was power from 9 in the morning to 11 at night. However, they wanted to make sure we were comfortable and had brought in a generator for us. They gave him instructions on use, shook his hand and most began to disappear through the front gate.

Abdullah told us that we could now take our rest in our room. We had three single beds, chairs, small stools and a shower off to the side. A few yards away were the school restroom facilities, otherwise known as "squatties." Aria and I had braced ourselves for this and knew that we could buck up and manage all that the week had to offer.

Later one of the men returned and asked us what we would like for dinner. Frankly, we did not know what to ask for, so we told him we would be happy with whatever he would want to bring us. (Risky, but culturally correct.) Soon he returned with roasted chicken, flatbread and a bag of fruit. Delicious indeed.

Soon after we ate, we were fairly tired, but we had one more errand to run. A driver in a truck arrived and escorted us to the school where we would be teaching. It was located a short jaunt away, but for our convenience and security, they drove us back and forth in a 4-door pickup.

This particular campus had been built by the British in 1956. I suspected everything still retained its original fixtures, paint, etc., with a few exceptions of some wall murals. John checked out the electrical outlets and found a suitable wall for projection.

... yet we were with people who woke up to just another day.

The men talked together while Aria and I stood to the side. This pattern would emerge for the rest of the week. However, we would have opportunity in the days to come to make some amazing friends.

Sunday morning marked the beginning of the week as well as a reminder about how radically our lives had changed in just 3 years. This Sunday morning was also Easter, a holiday deeply significant to us yet we were with people who woke up to just another day.

How privileged we were to be there–a privilege we did not take lightly. We began our day greeting each other with the traditional "He is risen. He is risen indeed" and started getting ready for our first day of teacher training. It was before 9 a.m. which meant there was no electricity so John kindly marched to the generator and turned it on so Pam the Diva could dry her hair. (I know. I know. My head would be covered anyway, but still it started out looking good. It was Easter.)

We received a knock at the door around 8 by one of the turbaned men bringing us our breakfast of *fuul* (beans, onions, garlic, tomatoes and cheese), bread, salad items, eggs and tea. We thanked the Lord for the food, the opportunity and the meaning of Easter. The food was amazingly good although we wondered who would make breakfast so early since Sudanese do not normally eat breakfast until 10 a.m. or so.

Around 8:30, more men arrived to escort us to the school. The caravan made its way for the quarter-mile drive depositing us at the front entrance. As we exited the truck, we were introduced to the governor who would be joining us for this morning's opening ceremonies. Wow, a governor.

Aria and I were careful to try to watch for cultural cues, but it was tough not knowing when to walk or when to talk or when to just stand and look at the ground. We were given instructions to head to the classroom where we began greeting all of the Sudanese teachers who were already in place at their desks.

Special chairs (sort of like Adirondack chairs with thick cushions) were placed at the front of the room for all the dignitaries. Aria and I still stood off to the side while the men placed John in the middle of the room with the governor.

The governor greeted the class with a 10-minute speech followed by a few of the education leaders. We did not have translation, but we could pick up a word here and there. I decided to just keep smiling through the entire thing. I think my face froze up half way through.

Once speeches were made, they waved goodbye and packed up their things. They left the room leaving us behind with 60 hopeful teachers staring back at us.

John and I hooked up the computer, projector and passed out books. We had everything ready to go when we realized that the electricity had not yet been turned on for the city. So John used this moment as a chance to introduce us and give a little overview of what would take place in the week.

The teachers that were participating were English teachers in the Sudanese government schools. However, most of had elementary levels of English which meant John needed to slow his pace down considerably and practice the art of restating. "Hello, Class. We will be learning about creating a lesson plan. We will talk together about making steps for teaching. Together we will discuss how to organize your materials to teach."

Our translator, Abdullah, was not anticipating the job of translating through the whole session so we did our best. John is extremely patient so he did not mind the blank stares or restating or the questions that would follow.

Slowly he began to introduce the material. At 10:30 a.m., one of the head teachers looked at John and said in accented English, "Time is finished." John looked at his clock and wondered what he meant. "Time to eat," the man said.

John dismissed the class and began gathering his notes for the next session. No one moved. The head teacher said, "You must go." So we walked out of the room and then all of the students followed. (It is apparently rude to leave before the teacher exits.)

Aria and I walked out of the room and began scouring the area for a bathroom. We could not find one anywhere on the campus. When we finally did one lady said, "Do not go in there. It is too dirty." Bad news.

One kind lady named Noor grabbed me by the hand and said, "Follow me." We walked off the campus toward a home next door through a desert path. Noor walked into the front of the house and greeted a young man sitting on the bed and promptly led me toward the bathroom. Talk about awkward.

"Hello, my name is Pam. I am from America and I have to go to the bathroom. Would it be too weird of me to walk into your house and use your facilities?"

However, no one seemed to think this was odd. After, we were introduced to all the kids in the home. To my relief, we discovered this was Noor's home. Whew.

We zipped back to the campus and headed toward the dining area. The women were separated from the men for eating. We walked in and the women began buzzing around us, "Where were you?" "Aren't you going to eat with us?"

Aria was whisked to one table and I was whisked to another. Five to seven women gathered around a bowl of *fuul* to share a meal. Flatbread was provided along with arugula and raw onions on the side.

> **I knew I had made a friend.**

As we stood around the bowl eating, one of the women began asking me questions about my family. She had a good grasp of English. Soon I noticed that many of the women were leaning in to hear my answers. In the North where we were located, not many foreigners made their way there. We were an amusement for sure.

We finished up with tea (one glass shared by all) and started walking back to class. Noor asked if we could have a picture together. I said I would love that. Class resumed and I smiled. I knew I had made a friend.

Our escort drove us back to our room where we rested for a couple hours before the next group of teachers arrived. We were exhausted. Trying to stay culturally sensitive for that many hours is a wipeout.

For the afternoon session John taught the same material as he had in the morning with 25 teachers and a much hotter room.

Sometimes John asked questions that would lean toward a particular answer; however, through their understanding of a second language he would receive a totally, out-of-the-blue answer. When this happened John would respond enthusiastically and say, "That is an idea!" The student would smile and nod.

The remaining class time was spent discussing classroom management. John spoke about the power of words and encouraged the teachers to use positive vocabulary in the classroom. One man said, "The only way Sudanese children can learn is with the stick!" We had heard about "the stick" before. Before desks, chairs, blackboards or even adequate books, every classroom is equipped with "the stick." John began exploring the topic of such punishment by asking them if they would like him to use the stick every time they answered incorrectly.

They did not, but that did not deter them from wanting to use it themselves when things got out of control in the classroom. The rest of the afternoon the teachers bantered with John about other ways to keep children engaged in the learning process. He concluded by affirming in a positive way each teacher who contributed to the discussion. They beamed. As he finished his session, he tied back his accolades to the teachers to their need to encourage their own students with words. Suddenly, a light bulb went on and we knew that something had shifted in the room. Genuine understanding had taken place; "the stick" equals fear, but respect equals learning.

We were driven back to our rooms. We received a new form of chicken for dinner as well as the news that soon they would be installing satellite TV for us. Satellite TV? Really? How about we make a trade? You take the TV in exchange for a simple, yet beautiful Western-style toilet. No? Okay, we will take the TV. How kind of them to think about us again. They could not imagine us going a week without watching soccer.

We ate our dinner as Aria read from the Bible about Jesus' resurrection. I thought about His willingness to leave the splendor of heaven to live among us. I thought about Emileigh and all the changes she had navigated over the year as a college freshman

94

and prayed that was having a good Easter. I looked at our humble surroundings and thanked the Lord for dear, generous village people who gave us their best from meager means.

Soon we were too weary to even finish watching the Bruce Willis movie on our newly installed TV. I prayed a prayer of blessing on our new friends, an Easter like no other and fell fast asleep.

Culture Cue

Read the history of your other-culture neighbor's home country. Your knowledge about her homeland will be a wonderful surprise in your next conversation. Try not to give opinions, however, about political situations as what is written does not necessarily reflect the sentiments of the local people.

24

Abdullah · Tell Me the Story
Listen Well, Share Hope

Our final evening up north, I picked up the flashlight, bug spray and toilet paper and made my way out to the squatty potties with dashed hopes that I could stave off a middle-of-the-night visit. The students knew that foreigners liked cold water in plastic bottles, so they gave us new bottles almost every 30 minutes throughout the whole day. By evening, my belly sloshed like I had swallowed the Nile.

I first opened the metal door of one of the stalls, sprayed bug killer, closed the door and waited a few seconds. I swung the door open and shown the flashlight on the floor. There were huge cockroaches everywhere. Most kept moving, but one looked up at me, leaned back on his antennae, lit a cigarette and smirked, "So what else have you got?"

> **I have to mentally prioritize my comfort way down the list of others' needs.**

I stomped and swirled the light, but they were nonplussed. It was me or the bugs. So far... Bugs 1. Pam 0. But Pam had to go to the bathroom. So I had to buck up, as they say, and hope the stubborn cockroaches knew the chorus of "Singing in the Rain."

Some ask, "How do you do it? How do you stand those conditions?" I will tell you. I do not. At least, not without getting the chills, shakes and reporting to John about what I had just endured. Somehow though there came a time when I realized that my purpose is bigger than a dirty bathroom and a few stubborn cockroaches.

I have to mentally prioritize my comfort way down the list of others' needs. Which is more important: the idea that these teachers may now consider using the stick less or that I have a pleasant bug-free experience? One may change generations of learning and perception; another will simply keep me from temporary whining.

The next morning, we packed our bags and began our series of goodbyes. The teachers we had spent the week with made a presentation of gifts, speeches and food. The governor came and presented us with a gift basket and a plaque of recognition.

We reciprocated with words of thanks, new dictionaries for their classrooms and a prayer of blessing.

As we left the village, the group waved. It was a different feeling from the first day we arrived. We now had friends, colleagues and standing invitations for return.

Our appointed liason, Abdelraheem, sat in the front seat with John while the women took their places in the backseat. I was fine with that. Aria and I were planning on a long nap on our way back to Khartoum.

John mentioned to Abdelraheem that it was our custom as followers of Jesus to pray and ask Him to bless our travels. Abdelraheem said, "This is a good idea!"

Aria prayed and we were on our way.

We had been on the road for about an hour when a *haboob* (sandstorm) came. The wind and sand pushed at the side of the truck and made visibility almost impossible. John had to slow to a crawl. We were in the middle of a desert. There were no places to stop. And stopping could mean tires are buried deep in sand. We pressed on.

John and Abdelraheem talked about the conference, the village, education and anything else that came to mind. Things became more personal as Abdelraheem spoke of his family and the dreams he had for them.

The wind began to gust more. John had to use both hands on the steering wheel to keep the truck on the road. Abdelraheem looked at Aria and said, "I think this is a good time to pray again!"

Aria laughed and said, "You are right!" So she did.

Abdelraheem relaxed a little bit after that and resumed chatting with John. John then turned to him and said, "You know, you're in the truck with three Christians. Do you have any questions you'd like to ask us?"

Without missing a beat Abdelraheem said, "Tell me the story!"

John replied, "Which story?"

"The story about Isa (Jesus) and Adam and Moses and everything!"

John laughed and said, "Well, with this sandstorm...you may just get to hear all of it!"

Several hours later we arrived at Abdelraheem's home where he insisted that we have a meal with his family before continuing onto Khartoum. Though they were not expecting us, they received us graciously and prepared an array of fruit, hardboiled eggs, cheese and bread.

As we said goodbye to Abdelraheem, he thanked John for being his friend and for telling him the story.

"I always wanted to know! Thank you!" he said.

The sandstorm had blown over and blue skies appeared. We waved to the family and made our way back to our home.

No fear, no comfort, no *cockroach* could or should keep me from a life this rich. I choose to step across the line and embrace this great adventure no matter where it may lead.

Culture Cue

Ask your other-culture friend to share his childhood stories. This will provide insight into his worldview and values.

Part 3:
The Village • Upper Egypt

25

Nasha • We Will Never Forget You
Seize the Day, Make the Most of Each Moment

"Where's the can opener?" I shouted.

"It's gotta be in here somewhere," John replied.

I continued my search and felt my growing frustration.

All. I. Want. To. Do. Is. Open. This. Stupid. Can. Of. Corn.

Suitcases and totes were scattered in the front room of our new apartment. We had spent the morning unpacking, but we were getting hungry and needed to take a break.

I rifled through a few more things willing the can opener to appear. No go. I went to Plan B. I chuckled out loud and thought that this is more like Plan W. How did we get here? Things were going so well…

John and I had just returned from an extended break in the U.S. We were preparing to return to Sudan for another term at the international school. Before we had left for America, we had received an open invitation with the Department of Education to continue the professional development among their government teachers throughout the entire country. The international school continued to thrive. We were finally getting our groove.

A few months prior to our return we began to hear rumblings of changes in the Sudanese government. Still we pressed on and arrived in Khartoum along with other devoted teachers ready to start the semester. John and I spent the first few days getting our apartment unpacked and in order. We were hopeful and anxious to renew our friendships.

However, it was not to be. Eleven days after we arrived in Khartoum, we repacked our bags and flew to Nairobi, Kenya. Three months later the teaching staff followed. Our time in Sudan had come to an abrupt, unexpected end...at least for a season. The separation of Sudan and South Sudan created an economic and political strain. The government tried a variety of methods to stabilize itself. One approach meant that most foreigners would be expelled over the next few months including us.

John and I held out hope that this sentiment would not last long and we would return. We talked with our colleagues, spoke with our family and prayed many prayers. Where should we go until then? What do we do now?

We landed in a small village along the Nile in Upper Egypt. The opportunities for professional development in education were ripe. The Nubians are a gracious, hospitable people and speak a similar Arabic dialect as the Sudanese. *Al-hamdulillah!* (Praise be to God!)

Which brings us back to the can opener. In our hurried "invitation" by the govern-ment to depart Sudan, we only packed a few things. I thought for sure that a can opener would be one of them. Not so.

> **We had lost our home, our jobs, our community, our friends.**

I felt tears welling in my eyes and knew that my angst was not about losing a gadget. The loss was so much deeper. We had lost our home, our jobs, our community, our friends. All in one fell swoop. More than that, our thoughts turned toward the dear people of Sudan who were left to face whatever this new future held.

The night we were to fly out from Khartoum, Nasha, a Sudanese school staff member, told John, "We don't want you to go. Thank you for coming here. We know it has not been easy. Thank you for caring about our people. We will never forget you."

John replied, "It has been our privilege to live here and to serve with you. We pray that God will bless you in the days ahead and that He will allow us to return one day."

"*Insh'allah. Insh'allah*," she said through tears.

Now to start over again. God, help us.

Culture Cue

Your other-culture friend may experience culture shock in her new setting. Unexpected tears may come or homesickness could be expressed. Be understanding. Everything for her is new and ofttimes overwhelming.

26

Salayla · You're a Tomato!
Laugh Often, Build a Friendship

"*Entee tomatum! Entee tomatum!*" ("You are a tomato! You are a tomato!") She yelled. I had just made it to the entrance of our village when I heard my friend, Salayla, calling me.

She motioned for me to come sit beside her in the shade of a mango tree. Her elderly mother, Rabah, lay on a straw mat next to her resting.

Salayla took my face in her hands and kissed both cheeks. Through a toothless grin she repeated, "You are a tomato!" Then she laughed as though she had just told the best joke. I laughed too and said, "When skin like mine is in a sun this hot, it turns very red!"

She laughed again and muttered, "Tomato, tomato..." She began yelling for her daughter who appeared from a colorful 2-story concrete home. Salayla said something in her Nubian language to her and the daughter rushed off.

Salayla adjusted her black *abiya* around her ample body and leaned back against the tree. She asked if I had children and if they lived with me. I told her that I had two daughters in college in America. She questioned to see if I had any sons and then prayed a quick prayer that sons would come to our family.

I asked about her family. Her husband had died long ago. She had several children, but I had a difficult time understanding exactly how many. I glanced at Rabah and asked how she was doing. Salayla laughed and said, "She complains all the time! Get me this! Get me that!"

Rabah piped up, "I have a headache. Get me some medicine!"

Salayla looked at me and shrugged, "See?"

Growing impatient, Salayla shouted in the direction of her home, *"Ya bit! Yallah!"* ("Girl! Let's go!") A few minutes later, her daughter emerged with a small silver tray and two small glasses of sticky, sweet steaming tea.

Salayla said, "This will help you not be so hot."

The temperature had reached 115 degrees and now this lady wanted to cook my insides as well.

"Drink! Drink!" she motioned.

I took the glass and began sipping. Ahhhh, this was *shy mazboot*. *Shy mazboot* is black tea with three heaping teaspoons of sugar. Its name literally means "perfect tea."

Salayla's daughter smiled when I complimented her tea-making skills. She started to sit down when Salayla shouted for her to go get Rabah some aspirin. The girl took off like a shot, and I smiled at the irony of Salayla's earlier comments about her mother.

She put her hand on top of mine and smiled.

We sipped and chatted. Salayla said, "See? I told you if you drink hot tea that it would cool you down."

I thought, *If I had a pop-up timer like those Thanksgiving turkeys in the U. S. had, mine would have popped by now.*

Salayla began rubbing her knee. She asked if I were a nurse and if so could I get her some medicine for the pain. I shook my head. I told her I was a teacher, but I was also a follower of Jesus and I would pray for her.

"Ah, Isa," she said. She clucked her tongue and gave me her medical history. She had knee problems, back problems and had *sugar* (diabetes). (If you are wondering, in this culture tea with three spoons of sugar three times a day does not count toward total sugar intake when holding to a diabetic diet.)

I shook my head in understanding and patted her leg. She put her hand on top of mine and smiled.

She then asked if I would like more tea. I thanked her, but declined. *Do you happen to have a tray of ice I could stick in my pants? No? Okay.*

We talked a bit longer and then I began making my parting comments. As is cultural, she protested, insisting I stay longer. I did, then started the departure remarks again. By the third time, she knew I truly must go. We hugged goodbye.

As I walked toward my home, she waved and said, "See you tomorrow, Tomato!" I could hear her continued cackling as I walked away.

Culture Cue

Westerners are known for having a large "bubble" of personal space. Many other-culture people do not have this same space requirement and may speak to you while standing very closely.

27

Sadik · The Bodyguard
Anticipate, Meet Kind People in Every Culture

Little by little, we built a new life making friends, equipping our home, increasing our Arabic vocabulary.

Okay. I will confess. I do not understand all of the Arabic that is going on around me during a conversation. In reality, it goes something like this:

You, *alksdjfla alskjdflkjalkjlkfjd* house *zxncvoiaelknadd* eat *aalkdjbpoiautpoit* daughter *alkdjbpoiazmnc* we go *alndoiajdnvoaijd,* yes?

At this point, I have three choices.

Choice #1: Nod my head in agreement. However, the last time I did this I inadvertently agreed to trade my daughter in marriage for 1,000 camels.

Choice #2: Stare blankly until they change the subject.

Choice #3: Ask them to repeat what they just said.

All have pitfalls from unplanned nuptials, to being perceived as "slow of thought," to sitting through another run at the conversation and perhaps picking up an additional two or three words.

All of this increases in difficulty exponentially when the Arabic speaker lacks proper enunciation due to lack of teeth. Which brings us to our dear friend, Sadik.

One day, John hailed a taxi and so began our relationship with Sadik. Sadik's appearance matched his taxi–older, a bit weather-worn and missing a few parts (teeth and air conditioning, respectively). He was a friendly sort and willingly drove us all around the area trying to locate the items on our list.

A friendship grew. Soon Sadik became "our guy" for any transport needs. He and John drank tea together, searched for the elusive can opener and shared family stories.

Sadik, a Nubian Muslim, had been a driver for a government official, but had been forced into retirement at age 60. He had a wife, a son and two daughters that he still needed to support so he fixed up a 1970s Russian-made car and went into the taxi business.

His kind, gentle demeanor and determination that we get the best local prices when we shop gave me confidence to strike out on my own with him to pick up a few things.

He saw in the rearview mirror that I had not understood everything.

As I got into his taxi, he asked about John and our daughters. I then inquired of his family. He began a long discussion that involved the words, "hospital," "stomach" and "Cairo."

He saw in the rearview mirror that I had not understood everything. Now I will say that a lot of our local friends will purposely slow down their speech and enunciate more clearly because they know we are listening carefully. Sadik has not adopted this practice. In fact, his story delivery is in direct connection to his driving style. Go real fast. Stop abruptly. Swerve. Regain speed.

Still puzzled with the story, I stopped at the first store and began checking my list. As I pushed the little shopping cart, I felt a tug. I looked up and Sadik smiled at me. He took the cart from me and said, "Mr. John isn't here. I will push the cart and watch out for you."

This was an extremely kind gesture, but also a terribly uncomfortable one. I tried to convince him that I would be just fine, but he reiterated, "Mr. John isn't here. I will make sure you are fine!"

So together we walked through the store. Sadik periodically clucked his tongue if he felt I were purchasing the wrong brand of something. I made it through the crowded, narrow aisles collecting glares and few things on my list.

Soon we returned to the taxi and he once again tried to explain his story. He pointed to his stomach, mentioned a hospital and said he had to go to Cairo. His hands gestured that there was a big problem and that he would be gone for 2 weeks.

I now began to piece together what he was trying to tell me. In language learning, this is called "sense making." We take the pieces that we do understand and fill in the gaps with our own paradigm.

I nodded with a concerned look and told him I understood. He leaned back in satisfaction.

When we arrived back at the flat, he carried my groceries to the door. John came out to greet him. As Sadik went to get the last few bags, I pulled John aside and said, "You have to pray for Sadik!"

John asked why. "He has stomach cancer and has to go to Cairo for treatment!"

"Oh, wow. Did he tell you that?" John asked.

"Yes, just now. He said he's going to be gone for 2 weeks. It sounds serious!"

"Okay. I'll talk with him," John said.

Sadik came with the last of the groceries. John invited him in to sit down and drink some water. As they sipped, John began asking about "the story."

I had to put the perishables away immediately so I could not hear everything that was being said. Soon I heard the door and peeked around the corner.

"Well?" I asked.

John shook his head. "Wow. You did *not* have the story."

It seems that Sadik did mention the words, "stomach," "hospital," and "Cairo" but not in the way I had pieced together.

Sadik had told John the same story he told me. However, John had had trouble also with a few of the words Sadik was using and charades ensued. Once Sadik included hand motions, John became crystal clear on the situation.

Sadik's oldest daughter had been married for 2 years and had not yet had a baby. She and her husband would be going through IVF at a hospital in Cairo.

John said that Sadik's explicit gestures helped in the lack of vocabulary.

"Ahhhhh, so glad I wasn't there for that part," I shivered.

However, now we knew how to pray. In Nubian culture, if a woman is unable to have a baby within the first 2 years of marriage, her husband is likely to divorce her and marry someone who can. It is rarely believed that the husband could be the one with the issue.

A few weeks later, Sadik, with a wide, toothless grin, told us the good news. His daughter was pregnant. We celebrated, too, that we understood what he said.

We were so thankful for his friendship, his kindness and his trust.

Yessireee! We were making our way. But just when you think you have figured it out…

Culture Cue

Learn the hierarchies in the other-culture family. In some cultures, the brother may need to give permission to his sister before she can visit a friend. Understanding this system will help you navigate invitations.

28

The Arborist · Tim-berrrrrrrrrrrr!
Remove Expectations, See Through New Eyes

With sweat trickling down the side of my red face, I declared it to be "autumn in Egypt." I loved living in Missouri where all four seasons are fully celebrated (sometimes in one day). In Egypt seasons are different. There is the hot season, the windy season, the really hot season and the cooler season. We were somewhere between the hot and windy season which (I had been told) led to the cool season.

Egypt weather is actually a bit different than the seasons in Sudan where one man told me, "In Sudan there are two seasons: summer and hell." I laughed really hard at that one.

So upon my declaration, I turned the A/C on high and made a pumpkin spice steamer from syrup we had carefully transported from the U.S. To Sudan to Kenya and finally to Egypt. We were still gathering necessary items for our kitchen, so I scrounged up a mug with a pharaoh on it left behind by a former tenant.

I sipped my hot drink while sorting through pictures I had taken in the U.S. last autumn. I had also been experimenting with sourdough bread recipes and had two loaves rising. A good morning.

Halfway through my drink, I heard loud thuds and chopping noises. Sometimes the men who operated the fishing boats loaded their equipment nearby so I did not think too much about it. Minutes later in my peripheral vision I caught something falling. That was not normal. I went to the window and saw a man in our tree standing on a branch jumping up and down on it. I was stunned. John was out of town and I had a man attacking our tree.

One of our neighbors, panicked over the tree decimation, knocked frantically on our door. It seems the landlord had hired an "expert" to trim the tree so they could see the water.

The neighbors explained that the tree they had requested be trimmed was not the tree that was being chopped. They asked the man in the tree to stop working. He had already done most of the "shaping," so he agreed to sit and drink some water while we all waited on the landlord to weigh in on this.

The "arborist" asked me for some water. He said, "But make it cold. I am not like others. I like to drink cold water when I work." He referred to a long-held belief that, if you drink cold water, you will actually become sick and get a cold. I appreciated his progressive attitude so I filled up his empty soda bottle with cold water.

He turned his attention to the tree. He climbed toward the top and went out on a limb. With a branch above him as a brace, he began hacking the limb he was standing on with his dull hatchet. I am not making this up.

My neighbors and I stood incredulously as he chopped and jumped and chopped and jumped trying to make the branch break. I had heard the saying, "Don't cut the limb you're standing on," but had never seen it performed in real life.

We were still in awe to be in a place with trees...

Just as the limb gave way, he held the top branch and swung himself to the trunk and shimmied down. He stood with his hands on his hips in proud accomplishment. He rounded the corner, knocked on the door and said, "More water."

I refilled his bottle and handed it to him. As he sipped, phone calls were made and discussions were held over the tree. The landlord's mother had told the man to chop it all down. That was his directive and that was his mission. The problem: it was the wrong tree.

Our neighbors hoped just to trim a few branches. The arborist adhered to the culture's belief that "more is more." This tree would be vanquished!

We hoped it could stay because of the afternoon shade it provided. We were still in awe to be in a place with trees, so removing any seemed almost criminal. After about 2 hours and several bottles of cold water it was decided: half of it would stay. The actual tree needing trimmed would be ignored completely this day and all the days to come.

John returned from his travels. As he walked down the sidewalk he saw the tree. "Do I even dare ask about this?"

I said, "You can, but you'll only end up shaking your head."

"I'm sure it's a good story. Tell me anyway."

I made us both a steamer, cut slices of sourdough bread (success!) and told him the story of the sad little tree whose autumn came swiftly and suddenly.

Culture Cue

Ask your other-culture friend how he greets someone in his home culture. Share with him how your culture greets.

29

Mokdee · The Little Engine That Could Not
Stay Fresh, Keep Your Circle Wide

I was half in half out of sleep when I caught myself reaching for a blanket. A blanket? We do not use blankets here. We never have anything more than a sheet on our bed. My fabulous new bedspread that I gave up several pounds and space for in my suitcase had been neatly folded on a shelf since our arrival. Each day I would look at it and sigh knowing that, if I did put it on the bed, it would be taken off once we went to sleep.

I was fully awake now and realized that the weather had shifted. Levels of "burn your brain" hot had dipped to what Missourians would call an "Indian summer day."

We decided to go for a long walk early through the city. We knew the desert heat would still eventually sap all the known liquids from our bodies by mid-afternoon. First we walked along the *corniche* (road along the Nile). We were greeted by the variety of *felucca* (sailboat) captains who hung out there looking for customers.

John knew a lot of them by name and he tried to divide our sailboat rides evenly among them. Sometimes they greeted us and would say, "Oh, how are you? Remember me? I missed you." It was a tactic they have learned about Westerners. We feel terrible when we cannot remember someone so we make up for it in boat rides. We got a little more savvy and actually knew who we *really* knew. (Still with me?)

One man, Mokdee, greeted us using similar phrases. He looked to be in his early 30s, average height, balding, Nubian and ready with a 4-toothed smile. He told us about his girlfriend in London. He told us his problem: he wanted her to come for a visit, but she was too afraid to come because of the trouble in Egypt. John nodded his head in understanding, wondering where this conversation was headed. We had just met the guy. Mokdee said, "Other cities may have trouble, but not here." John agreed. Our little section of the country for the most part had remained calm.

Mokdee continued, "She is very beautiful, you know?" He nudged John with his elbow. I tried to keep from rolling my eyes. "I want her to know it's safe."

John said, "Yes, we are telling our friends that it is fine to travel here now."

Mokdee said, "Yes, but if my girlfriend could hear it from you…"

Now we understood. He wanted John to call his girlfriend and assure her that it would be fine for her to come.

John said he understood, but Mokdee's girlfriend would need to talk with her family to make that decision.

Mokdee nodded and asked for a final time if we were well. John assured him we were and we bid our goodbyes.

Our relationship with Mokdee grew. He always had an angle, some get-rich scheme and he wanted John to be a part of all of them. John would discuss with him the pros and cons of certain ventures, pointing out that honest money earned is the best route. Mokdee did not always agree.

> **Friendship can be stretching…and bone-jarring…and neck-snapping, but ultimately it is worth it.**

A few months into the friendship, John received a call from Mokdee. He had a new car and wanted to take John for a ride. He told John he would meet us at our gate and that he would be the one "with the shiny red car." John said, "This should be an adventure."

Right on time, Mokdee had arrived as promised. Mokdee fired up the engine and tried to accelerate. The car lurched and stopped. John observed a few problems quickly.

1. Mokdee had never driven a stick shift before.
2. Mokdee had never *driven* before.
3. Mokdee did not know anything about cars.
4. Mokdee did not think any of the above three issues were issues.

Mokdee turned the key again and stepped on the gas. He attempted to put the car into first. The sound of grinding gears reverberated throughout the neighborhood and a few people began to fix their attention on the car.

He called down curses on this "worthless piece of junk" and assured John they would be on their way in no time. More lurches, more gears missed, more curses...the engine had now flooded.

Mokdee popped the hood, put his hands on his hips and began staring intently at the engine. John had been raised around car engines and knew a thing or two about them; however, Mokdee felt sure he could figure this out.

Two other men came and also stood with their hands on their hips staring at the engine. I thought, *It is the same everywhere.*

One man worked on the engine while the other tried to turn over the engine. They yelled back and forth tinkering with things until the engine roared to life. Mokdee smiled and told John they were ready to go.

Mokdee tried to slip the gear into first, but found third and began revving up the small incline. The loudness of the engine had most neighbors' attention, but Mokdee could not be dissuaded. He proudly drove slowly with several lurches through the village waving as he went. John wondered if they would be able to drive straight to a chiropractor.

Mokdee, first, drove very cautiously and at incredible turtle speeds. As he gained confidence, he took on the Indy driver approach while John clutched the dash and asked God for one last chance at life.

He asked John why we did not have a car. John replied, "Taxis here are plentiful and cars are expensive to maintain." Mokdee nodded in agreement. He said, "Yes, something is always breaking. Always more money!"

He thought a car might impress his girlfriend in London enough to return. It did not. Now the car needed more repair. Mokdee told John of another scheme that was "sure to work" this time.

John advised Mokdee against it. "But there is no tourism and I can't read!" he protested.

Ah, a large percentage of Nubians and Upper Egyptians are illiterate or low-functioning literate. Many must join their families in working at a young age to bring in income. We came, in part, to address this very issue.

John continued working with Mokdee and being a true friend though it was hard at times. His "great ideas" would sometimes even be looked upon by the villagers as suspect.

Still, asking God for wisdom John would periodically meet with him. Sometimes the red car would swing by and pick him up. At other times, John met him at a predetermined location to avoid another Jeff-Gordon-without-the-skills experience.

Mokdee never disappointed. He continued to strive to better his situation. We appreciated that in him.

Friendship can be stretching...and bone-jarring...and neck-snapping, but ultimately it is worth it. It keeps our circle wide and our perspective fresh. Mokdee did that for us. We never knew what was coming next.

Culture Cue

Remember your opinion does not reflect all of the Western world, nor does his opinion reflect all of his culture.

30

Sena · Loving Her People
Go Beyond Yourself, Leave a Legacy of Love

In January 1900, a German man and his son created a center of operations in Aswan as a local school and as a base reaching into Sudan. In 1906, a Swiss doctor joined and began offering medical services to the local people.

Each year since then, *al Germaniyya*, has served the local people of this city faithfully for over 100 years through affordable medical care, life-skill workshops, children's programs, a bookstore and more.

This light of hope has been shining in this difficult area of Egypt where diseases are rampant and resources are few. We were privileged to work with some of the dedicated staff and come alongside them as they expanded their reach throughout the area.

One such staff member is Sena. In her early 40s, Sena is a devout Egyptian Christian who loves fiercely and serves endlessly. Her English-speaking abilities bridged the gap in my Arabic which assisted our conversations to develop into a sincere friendship. We talked about hairstyles, where to find jeans and swapped recipes. But mostly she talked about her people and how we could serve them.

Sena oversees clinics and workshops held in the surrounding villages such as the one we live in. Sometimes she will schedule soccer clinics or eye exams or English classes depending on the needs and requests of those in the village.

She called John and said a group of teachers in our village would like training. He readily agreed, took on "beaver mode" and began to plan. (This is his custom for just about everything in life. I really love this about him…most of the time.)

We knew what topics we would teach, but what we did not know was:
-the location of the training
-who would come
-how many would come
-how many days it should run

One has to learn to live with nebulous here or you will die young of a stress aneurism.

Sena said she would arrange everything and that we should show up the following Monday at 5 p.m.

"Where?" John asked.

"In the village mosque," she said, nonchalantly.

Apparently, there are big rooms inside that the village elders call "The Association." Basically, all village life for anything transpires there. John and I smiled. Wow.

Monday arrived and we made the short walk to the mosque. The door was locked. No one was around except several kids who were frozen in place staring at us. We waited for a bit and then called Sena to make sure we had the right time, day and place. No answer. Not a good way to start a seminar.

I silently thanked Jesus for His incredible creativity in demonstrating His love to all people.

Right at 5 p.m., 2 vehicles pulled up and a crew of Egyptian 20-somethings exited, smiling and chatting all at the same time. Sena had sent them to help us. Amazing. One of the men who worked in the mosque arrived, greeted us and unlocked the door. He took us to an upstairs room and showed us where we would be teaching.

The crew began setting up the projector, screen, moving tables and preparing the room. I paused to think how strange this was. Christians setting up teaching inside a mosque in a predominately Muslim country. I silently thanked Jesus for His incredible creativity in demonstrating His love to all people.

Everything was ready. We asked about the printouts for the teachers and were told they were not ready yet.

"Tomorrow," he said. Again, "flexible pants" were a necessity.

Slowly, but surely a few timid women from our village entered the room. Since this was a teacher development workshop, I had been under the impression that teachers would attend. And some did, but it was about 50/40/10. Others who came were mothers who wanted to know how to assist their children in their schoolwork. Still others were curious to see what the foreigners would say or do.

The first night we had 33 adults. Of the 33, we had a mix of Egyptian Christian men and women, Nubian Muslim women, a Sudanese Muslim woman, some Egyptian Muslim women and Westerners. (This does not include two babies, three toddlers and two middle schoolers.) As days progressed, we settled into an average of around 24 and added several more Muslim men and various crawling children.

Educational terms are difficult even as a first-language speaker, so we were grateful we had a translator who jumped in to help us explain the materials.

Around 7 each night of the training, a small boy walked in carrying a silver tray loaded with tiny glasses of hot steaming, heavily sugared tea. Teatime waits for no one here. He served everyone and then disappeared. No one had told him to bring it.

This particular workshop included "Lesson Plans," "Classroom Management," "Learning Styles" and "Teacher Professionalism." The participants received the information with enthusiasm. Most of this material was completely new to them. Teachers in government schools receive little in the way of support and resources. They try to manage a class size of 60-plus with limited space and shared textbooks.

I taught them some classroom cheers meant to be used to

encourage student success. They loved them so much they began giving John and me cheers after every section we taught. Their favorite was "The Roller Coaster" even though we had to show them a youtube video of an actual roller coaster so they knew what it was.

At the end of the six-session workshop, all who attended every session received a Certificate of Completion. I made *bupcakes* (cupcakes) and some of Sena's staff had juice and other sweets ready. We took class pictures, ate, celebrated and received one more roller coaster cheer before we departed.

We asked them to complete a survey for feedback. They were kind in their remarks, indicating they would like future training. One said that "John's smile made it all worth while." (I have repeated that phrase a few times since then. It amuses me so.) But before anyone could get prideful, one participant said, "It just made me want to sleep all the time." I am hoping something was lost in the translation.

After the workshop ended, we would see some of the students who had been present at the training. They warmly received us. It became a turning point for us and how we were perceived now as one of them.

Sena thanked us for our work, but we were the ones who were thankful. She had built the relationships. She had made numerous calls and attended lengthy meetings to make it all happen. More than that, she simply had a heart for people.

Our actions and choices will either create a path for those following or a wall that will have to be climbed.

I wonder if those few brave souls in the early 1900s knew that their grit and determination would create such a wide door for those following 100 years later? I wonder if we (present day) understand that our actions and choices will either create a path for those following or a wall that will have to be climbed?

Sena and others like her pave the way by not giving up, by going to remote places, by simply showing care and offering hope.

They want their people to thrive, to grow, to have opportunities. The people in the villages know it and return her love in spades.

Thank you, Sena. We are grateful to have served with you and to witness such selfless servanthood. May your dream of spreading love and hope to those you serve be fulfilled in Egypt and beyond.

Culture Cue

Laugh with your other-culture friend. You will both make mistakes. Be gracious, forgiving and have a sense of humor!

31

The *Imam* • You Must Come!
Teach Someone To Learn, Give Him a Future

Upper Egypt boasts a rich history of Pharaonic tombs, ancient garrisons and soaring monuments. Occasionally, we would host friends who would want to visit these places and we would gladly oblige. I have been an amateur Egyptologist since I discovered King Tut in a volume of my *Childcraft: The How and Why Library.*

One particular archeological site we would visit is still an "open dig." Every winter, archeologists from around the world come and work layer by layer revealing five levels, 6,000 years of civilization.

We happened on a true-to-life Indiana Jones during one visit. He even wore a fedora! He introduced himself and gave us a little background of the location. "Dr. Jones" said that this dig wasn't "sexy archeology" like King Tut's tomb but still very important to the understanding of ancient cultures.

He had a wish that the whole area could be turned into a working site including those locations that had "modern" homes. This, of course, did not sit well with those living in said homes. An ongoing tension of sorts developed and Dr. Jones kept to "his side" of the site.

Dr. Jones concluded his talk and made it clear that he was indeed not for hire. This meant we would need a tour guide to give us the pertinent facts we so desired. I discovered "the" guy who knew all about the area. He had been born there, studied ancient history and served as a tour guide. We will call him "Ali."

The previous guy I had hired walked around and pointed saying in heavily accented English, "Thees (pointing to an ancient temple) ees veddy, veddy big and veddy, veddy old." The tour continued and he said (pointing to a smaller temple), "Thees ees not veddy big, but veddy, veddy old." Similar descriptions were given throughout the entire tour.

John and I developed a friendship with Ali. We met his wife and daughter, drank tea in his home and discussed many topics. We discovered he was also an *imam* (pastor) of a local mosque.

I met Ali one morning with a visiting friend for a tour. He greeted my friend and then asked how John was doing. I said that John sent his greetings, but he had work and would be unable to join us.

"What is he working on?" he asked.

"He's developing a curriculum for a village preschool."

Ali smiled and said, "This is good! I am very worried about our preschool!"

"Why is that?" I asked.

An imam and a Christian coming together to stop terrorism. God was doing marvelous things.

"Because the teachers only teach the children to rock back and forth and recite the Qur'an. They do not teach the children how to learn, how to think. These children grow up listening to others, but not their fathers. If the children learn how to think they won't blindly accept every idea given to them. You tell John that if he wants to stop terrorism then he must come and start a preschool in my village!"

I am sure my mouth dropped open. I could not believe my ears. An imam using the "t" word demanding that we start a preschool in his village.

He continued, "You tell John to come see me today!"

I assured him I would and we continued with the tour. As my

friend and I waved goodbye to him, he said, "Don't forget! Tell John to come!"

I reported what had happened when I got home. "Wow," was all John could say.

He went to Ali's house and discussed details. Ali was definitely on board. He just needed to clear it with the village elders. He asked John to give him some time.

Our friendship with Ali was a gift. In his 60s, he outran both of us when leading us up and down the archeological sites. If I asked for the 1-hour tour, he would still give 3-hours worth of information, but we heard it as we ran from point to point.

An *imam* and a Christian coming together to stop terrorism. God was doing marvelous things.

Culture Cue

Avoid culture-specific examples or humor with your other-culture friend until you can determine if she has understanding. Also, be careful that the conversation does not create an "us-them" situation.

32

Samia · A Widow's Plight
Find Common Ground, Refresh Each Other

It is customary for the women in our village to gather in late afternoon to visit with one another before starting dinner. My friend, Sarah, and I were walking home one day when we came upon Sarah's friend, Samia. Samia greeted us each with a handshake and a kiss on each cheek.

We exchanged pleasantries when Samia asked if we would like to join her for tea the next day. We agreed on a time and went on our way.

Sarah and I discussed "Glamorous Samia" on the way home. She had gotten this nickname from us because of the multiple women in the village with this name. When trying to differentiate between them, Sarah would say, "You know, Glamorous Samia!"

"Oh, yes!" I'd say knowing exactly who she meant.

Glamorous Samia had a beautiful smile, light brown eyes lined in charcoal and always wearing a brightly colored headscarf. We were about the same age and I marveled at her ability to look so put-together. I, on the other hand, looked very...tomato-ish.

I met Sarah the next day and we made our way down the street toward a house that we thought was Samia's. We looked around the building, but all the doors were shut and no one was around.

Thankfully a woman and small boy appeared around the corner. I inquired where Samia lived and she pointed down a different street.

We took our plate of thank-you-for-inviting-us cake and began walking from house to house looking for anything that would indicate we were close. Soon a few women spotted us and we asked them about Samia. They pointed up toward a balcony where Samia was smiling and waving.

We walked through a small wooden door up the concrete steps into a simply furnished home. Samia greeted us along with her visiting daughter and two grandchildren, ages 2 and 10 months.

She had her daughter bring out two chairs on the balcony while the remaining folks sat on a bed already in place. I thought, *This is a good idea. It never rains here so why not make the balcony another bedroom?*

Samia brought a bowl of fruit and two cups of steaming tea with fresh mint leaves. *Shy koshary* has loose tea leaves, so it is wise to stir in the sugar and then wait until it all settles. If you do not, you risk a mouthful of bits and brown teeth.

We were all mothers with love for our children in common.

The sugar had a few ants in it. I deftly attempted to dodge them while scooping and distracting the hostess with questions. I think I succeeded. (John said that poached ants are quite tasty.)

We tried to understand all the Arabic that was flying around us. We managed to catch some phrases that allowed the conversation to flow back and forth. Sarah spoke of her family and I told her about mine. We were all mothers with love for our children in common.

Samia pulled out a stack of photos of herself, her daughters and her friends. Photos are a big deal in this culture and Photoshop is *huge*. If one image of a person is good, then four of them in a collage in front of the Eiffel Tower must be great. After we looked through the collection, Samia told us that her husband died 17 years ago. Since then it has been just her and her three girls.

She shook her head and said, "No sons. *Doonia*." ("It is the world.") No sons in this society make it very difficult for Samia's future since the daughters once married usually live with the husband's family.

She put away the photos and came back with a small silver plate with salt and cowrie shells on it. Her daughter asked if we wanted to participate. I told her that I was unsure of what she was doing. She explained that Samia would toss the shells, salt and tea leaves then predict the future for my daughters, i.e. who will they marry, how many babies will they have, etc.

I thanked her but told her we pray to God and He guides our days and our lives. They both smiled and said, "*Kwyees! Kwyees!*" ("Good! Good!"). Samia put away the plate and offered us more tea. We thanked her politely, played with the grandchildren a bit more and then began to make our exiting statements.

I told her, that when we returned for tea the next time, I would bring pictures of my family and hometown in America. She was pleased.

She shook our hands and kissed us both as we made our way down the steps. Samia yelled down to us to be sure and come back. We waved and told her we would. Three women from three different countries yet we found common ground around a teapot. We are more alike than we often think.

Culture Cue

Do not ask, "Which do you like better? This country or your old country?" Every culture has positives and negatives. Making your other-culture friend choose can feel disloyal to both.

33

Samir · Shall We Dance?
Celebrate, Share in the Joy

Wedding season in our village began after Ramadan and before the start of the school year. The celebrations usually took place Thursday through Sunday starting at around 10:00 p.m. and lasting until the wee hours of the morning.

Our taxi driver friend, Sadik, had invited us to join him and his wife at a wedding. We had a good time and told him so. He invited us to join him for another wedding the following weekend.

I am all for getting out in the culture and being among the people. After all, that is the point. However, along with all this opportunity comes some pretty debilitating "bonuses" that happen. Take this wedding, for example.

Sadik arrived with his car at 9:30 p.m. John wore his *jalibaya* and I wore some of my blinging American clothes. (My *abiya* was dirty.) Sadik told us he needed to pick up some family members on the other side of town before the wedding. We made it through the traffic, noticing that the streets were filling up with other wedding parties along the Nile's edge at local clubs.

After about 15 minutes we arrived at Snob Café (real name) where we were supposed to meet his family. Sadik made a few inquiries and found they had not arrived yet. He waited about 10 minutes and then told us they would come later.

We went back across town to a reception hall we had not been to before. You could hear the music pounding as we approached the entrance. Sadik's wife spotted us and waved us over. She greeted me with four kisses and took my hand. Sadik pointed to one door and told me that the women were in there. I told John goodbye knowing we would be separated the rest of the evening as is custom.

At the door we were greeted by this cute little old man who had been at the last wedding. Samir was in his 60s and had a toothless smile. Sadik told us he was deaf and mute, but he communicated through his own version of sign language. It seems he attends all the weddings he can so he is an expected fixture at these events.

Samir smiled broadly as we walked in, handed me a juice box and pointed to the front. I took the juice and followed his directions.

Sadik's wife led me to a group of benches near the front of the stage where the disc jockey was set up. Lights were flashing from a giant decorative heart overhead. The DJ had Amr Diab blaring and approximately 1.3 million children were running around in their best clothes having a really good time.

Many guests were already present (at least 300). It seemed that all 600 eyes were following me as I made made my way to the women's section. I was greeted by two women who looked to be mother and daughter. They shook my hand curtly until I greeted them in Arabic. Then their eyes lit up and they gave me a kiss and insisted I sit down. (I guess all that brain-numbing language study does pay off.)

I settled in as the staring subsided, when Samir appeared at my row. He smiled and walked toward me. He pointed to the stage and began to dance. Then he gestured that I join him.

All eyes were now back on me as we had this exchange. I froze. Sadik's wife told him (or rather motioned) that I did not want to dance. He persisted. More eyes turned toward us. His arms began to flap wildly. I held my ground. Sadik's wife finally took him by the arm and told him that I would not be dancing and that he should go back to juice box duty. I breathed a sigh of relief.

The women patted me on the back as if to say, "It's okay. We understand." The music continued to play as we all waited for the bride and groom to arrive. The clubs stay open only until 12:30 a.m., which means the bride and groom have to arrive before that if they want to have any party time.

It was now 11:45 p.m. and I asked the lady next to me if she thought the wedding couple would make it in time. "*Insh'allah*," she says. Shortly after, live drums began to play and a troop of young men dressed in matching outfits led the way for the bridal party. They had arrived in time. Everyone rose to their feet and began clapping.

The bride's mother walked ahead of them throwing candy into the crowd. Alongside her was a boy off the street holding a handful of Spongebob balloons he hoped to sell to the gazillion children.

The couple danced their way to the front of the stage where they took a seat on the ornately decorated bench. At this point the wedding guests begin to make their way to the front to congratulate the couple. I waited for John and Sadik to come so that we could go together. However, Sadik did not see us so he and John went alone.

Sadik's wife took my hand and told me we could go up also. Just then Samir returned. He thought I was ready to dance. I told him no thank you and had supporting motions to reinforce the idea. He then understood we were going to greet the bride and groom so he took it upon himself to part the way. It was of Moses-like proportion. He began swatting his arms back and forth, yelling at the crowd in an indistinguishable voice. However, they seemed to know what was happening and parted like the Red Sea.

All eyes were on me as we walked through on dry land. We made our way up the stairs, but Samir still was not finished. He began pushing on my back so that I would get to the front. I was trying to not make a spectacle and to be respectful of those already in line. Samir did not see it that way. He moved two small children and handed me to the bride's mother who in turn handed me to the bride. I was now 2 inches from the bride (one I did not know). I gathered my composure and congratulated her. She was as surprised as I was, but graciously accepted my greetings.

I turned to walk back down the stairs where Samir awaited me. He cleared the path toward the dance floor, but I quickly skirted my way back to my seat. Sadik's wife had somehow survived the frenzy with me and had arrived back at the same time.

A lady handed me a bag with two bottles of Dasani water in it. "For you," she said. I thanked her for her thoughtfulness. The greetings waned a bit so the groom made his way to his group of friends near the front of the stage and began to dance. They hoisted him on their shoulders, threw him up in the air and danced all around him.

Samir saw this as his moment, jumped up on stage and began dancing wildly. He tried to make eye contact with me to join him, but the fuchsia satin curtains held deep fascination for me.

The bride danced with her friends up on stage, although briefly. The heat was still quite oppressive and she had on many layers. (Here the bride does not carry a bouquet but a decorated fan which is way more practical.)

I'm the only Christian in the room.

I sipped water, tapped my foot to the beat when I noticed someone poking my back. I turned to see who it was and was greeted by a girl about 12. She smiled and said, "Whassyourname?" I introduced myself and asked her hers. Soon word got around that the foreign lady was approachable. Now a continuing stream of pokes, giggles and handshakes followed.

A few adult women also came by to greet me and say hello. They were extremely kind and gracious, but always with the glint in their eye that says, "What is she doing here?"

It is a novelty to invite a foreigner to social events. We received many invitations to occasions. But was that why I am here? To be some sort of a strange Paris Hilton? Of course not. It is far too difficult and stressful to make this a full-time occupation for the sake of just being wanted.

Being a minority everything all the time in every situation is awkward and tiring. The staring, which is not impolite in this culture, can be brutal. At events like these, I'm the only one not wearing a head covering. I'm the only one not brown-skinned. I'm the only non-Egyptian. I'm the only Christian in the room.

Wait. I am the only Christian in the room. I scanned through the crowd and looked at each individual. Samir was still dancing. Sadik's wife sat close to me. Sadik and John were with the men on the other side of the room. The children were gathered around me. I paused and breathed a prayer for each one.

"Jesus, be real to them," I prayed, "and please let Samir find a new dance partner."

Culture Cue

Know that time may have a very different meaning to your other-culture friend. When you agree to meet at 10 a.m. for coffee, she may understand through her cultural lens that you mean sometime in the morning. Talk about these things and be flexible.

34

Farhat · Middle-East Maxine
Take the Risk, Love the Difficult

One of the funniest characters Hallmark ever created is Maxine. Maxine is a cranky, old lady who always sees the glass half-empty, cracked and leaking. I have said on more than one occasion that I might indeed be the personification of her if not for Jesus reminding me to be kind. It seems the spirit of Maxine lives in more than one culture. I believe I had met her Middle-Eastern self right in our small Nubian village. Except Maxine goes by the name of Farhat.

Farhat lived alone in a small mud brick home near ours. She sat on the stoop by her front door every morning watching the other villagers going about their day. She said little, watched much and sometimes chased children with a stick if they got too close.

As I was returning from errands one day, I stopped to greet her with the traditional two kisses on each cheek. After the normal, "How are you? How did you sleep? Are you doing well? How was your morning? How was your afternoon? You are doing well?" she then asked, "Where have you been?"

I said I have been here. I asked, "Where have you been?"

She clucked her tongue, "I am here! I am always here! You think I go anywhere?! I don't go anywhere! Ever!"

Well, I am glad that was settled.

I told her it would make me so happy to sit and drink tea with her.

She asked, "Why?"

I said, "We have had tea together before and I miss you."

She smiled and then went serious. "My house or yours?"

"My house would be fine. Why don't you come by tomorrow afternoon with Durrah" (a mutual friend)?

"What time?" she asked gruffly.

"2 o'clock, okay?"

She paused and clucked her tongue again. "Okay. Okay."

After some back and forth deciding if this really was a good time, she agreed.

The next day at 2:07 p.m., she knocked. I opened the door and ushered her into our living room.

"Where's Durrah?" she asked.

"I don't know. I thought she was coming with you."

She mumbled to herself with words I did not understand. It was probably better that I did not.

I offered her some raspberry iced tea. Definitely not what she was expecting, but I thought she might like it.

"What is this?" she asked.

"Tea," I said.

"No, it's not."

"It is iced tea."

I thought she would roll off the couch. No Durrah and now iced tea. It was not that I was trying not to follow culture; I wanted to give her something new to try that was from America. I thought she might like the experience. Now I was not so sure.

The rule is: If you do not know the word, it will not help to say it at another speed or volume.

I offered her a brownie and some fresh pomegranate. She said she would eat it later.

We chitchatted a while as I tried my best to keep up with her Arabic. If I asked what a word meant, she just said it louder and shook her head in disgust. It made me laugh. It reminded me of myself a few times when I have tried to help others understand English by talking louder and slower. The rule is: If you do not know the word, it will not help to say it at another speed or volume.

I heard a knock and opened it to a flustered Durrah. She began apologizing profusely for being late. I told her I was happy to see her. She presented me with a bag of oranges and made her way to the couch.

Farhat was less forgiving. She began telling Durrah, "You're late! We said 2 o'clock and it's almost 2:30. What were you doing? We said 2 o'clock!"

Durrah, a younger woman, took the chastisement gracefully. Once Farhat had said her piece she resumed the conversation with me. Funny.

Durrah immediately took the photo album containing Emileigh's wedding photos and began commenting. Farhat had already seen them so she began nibbling on the brownie I had set in front of her earlier.

After a few more minutes, Farhat said that she had to go. She had to go to the doctor and she did not want to be late. She emphasized "late" while looking at Durrah.

I walked her to the door and told her how happy I was that she came. She gave me a half grin and I sensed I had gained her approval if begrudgingly.

Durrah finished the photo albums and drank the iced tea with enthusiasm. (Farhat had tried a sip, but declared the weather too cold to finish it. It was 90º.) Durrah then needed to leave. I thanked her for coming and welcomed her back anytime.

I closed the door and began cleaning up. Farhat is what my mother would call "a tough ol' bird," but she let me see a glimpse of the woman inside for just a moment.

A few weeks later I passed her house and saw a group of goats near her door. (Herd? Passel? Congress? Anyway.) Farhat had a stick and was prodding the goats toward a pile of trash.

I asked, "Oh, did you get new goats?"

She responded tersely, "Yes, I have goats. Can't you see that they're goats?"

Not to be dissuaded, I pressed on. "Are you raising them?"

Now by her response I had grown a third eye. "Of course, I'm raising them! I'll feed them 'til they're big and then…" She made a gesture across her throat indicating the future demise of said herd.

Then she smiled and pointed out a baby goat. She fed him a piece of banana and patted him on the head. "This one won't be eaten for a long time."

Good news for Junior.

She asked me if I wanted to drink tea together. We went inside her home where she directed me to the *saloon* or what we might call the formal living room. Ornate gold brocade cushions cover simple sofa-shaped concrete. Layered blue drapes with gold tassels hung over the windows. She placed a small wooden table near the sofa and told me to sit.

I followed her instructions. Soon she rounded the corner with one small glass of hot tea. She told me she had already put the sugar in. I thanked her, took the cup and asked where hers was.

She said, "I never drink tea at this time of day. It would keep me up all night!"

So why then…? I could have….

I thought at least she wants to have tea with me. I made a joke and asked her if I should go get some of my iced tea for her. She frowned and said that tea made with ice is *wahesh* (ugly). I like a woman who speaks her mind.

I thanked her and walked toward the door. She gave me a hand gesture to wait and reappeared with a gift bag. I started to thank her for it, but she took my arm and led me out the door telling me that she would see me tomorrow.

Once home, I looked inside the bag. As it was nearing Christmas, she had purchased a small porcelain jewelry box for me with Santa Claus on it. I wondered where she had found such a thing in a Muslim-majority location.

Moved deeply by this gift, I placed the box in a special spot. It reminds me of Farhat and all the Maxines of this world who love and want to be loved. We just have to have the time and tenacity to see them, truly see them.

Culture Cue

Talk about spiritual matters. Many cultures consider spiritual discussions as common as the weather. To not talk about it seems odd to most.

35

Musa · You're Engaged!
Join the Fray, Participating Precedes Belonging

"Y ou are invited," he began shyly, "to my engagement party on the last day of *Eid*."

"Engagement party!" John exclaimed, "You're getting engaged?"

Musa gave a half smile and said, "Yes."

We both burst into exclamations of congratulations for our dear friend who had not mentioned a word about any particular girl until now. He is rather shy and I suspect he knew it would cause great attention.

We agreed to come. John said, "I will even buy a new *jalibaya* for the occasion."

Musa told us he would send a driver to our home to pick us up on the evening of the event. We thanked him for his thoughtfulness. Paved streets do not usually have signs and dirt paths in winding villages become even more difficult to navigate.

The days of *Eid* passed festively as Muslims celebrated the end of Ramadan. The *souq* (market) had been closed for the holiday, so John and I had to wait until the night before Musa's party to purchase our new outfits.

John is very much a "search and destroy" type of shopper, so we entered the *souq* at the exact shop we needed. Purchased said *jalibaya* for him and *abiya* for me within 30 minutes. Done and done.

We knew these parties typically run long into the night, so we had already thought it best to take a nap prior to the big hoopla.

Around 9:30 p.m. we received a call from Musa saying the driver should be arriving soon. A friend of Musa's had agreed to share his car and pulled up right on time (within an hour of any given time is *very* punctual).

We rode across town to a new section that we had not visited before. Our village is next to a city that is half a million people, so there is a lot we had yet to explore. The roads became alleys and the alleys become paths until we were in the correct area of the village where the width of a car would no longer fit. He said, "We'll park here."

Our driver directed us up the alley toward loud music and flashing lights. People in the village had already begun to line the path, and we had to walk the gauntlet. Everyone was very friendly, greeting us along the way, but also declaring that *khawajat* (foreigners) were coming.

As we approached the party, we evaluated who was where. The men were seated in a side alley with benches; the women were inside the bride's family home. John and I said our goodbyes and I put on my brave pants as I entered the room full of women.

> **I was especially conscious of the fact that everyone watched me.**

I was immediately greeted by a girl about 20 who took my hand, introduced herself and directed me to sit on a padded bench. Soon more women arrived. All greeted one another while catching a side glance of me. They came around, shook my hand and took their place in the provided seating. We waited. Music played in the background, kids danced in the middle and the women spoke quietly to one another.

Around 11:30 p.m., an aunt of the host family walked in with a large tray of food and began passing out plates to all the guests. I was one of the first ones served. My plate contained white sauce lasagna, zucchini stuffed with rice, pieces of beef, bread and *tahina* (sesame dip). No goat eyeballs were present on the plate.

All of it was delicious. I was especially conscious of the fact that everyone watched me and wanted to know what I thought of the food. I made sure I complimented the food many times loudly.

Musa's mother greeted me and insisted I eat more. She poured a glass of 7-up for me and told me to "Eat! Eat!"

John in the men's area was also eating. However, he reported a different scene: the men ate at long tables, they were silent. They would eat about half their food and then get up and walk away.

I am afraid that type of system would kill the women who were talking, laughing and asking each other about their day.

The plates were collected and we chitchatted some more. I would answer a question and it would be passed along the room until everyone smiled and nodded. Then another question. I suppose it was a good diversion because the bride-to-be had not yet arrived from the *coiffure* (hair stylist).

It is tradition for the bride and her bridesmaids to go to the hair salon for updos, henna and makeup. This is an all-day and mostly all-night procedure.

Around 1 a.m., one woman announced that the bridal party had arrived.

Let's get this party rolling, I thought to myself.

We exited the house and gathered in the center of two inter-secting streets. Arabic pop music pumped through the air making conversation impossible. John pulled out his earplugs, a habit from his former audio engineering days.

Musa stood nervously dressed in a Western suit and tie. The whole look shocked me. I thought he would be in a dressy *jalabaya*, but instead he had on our type of clothing. What?

The bride wore a bright fuchsia dress that was completely bedazzled. Her hair had been styled beautifully with curls and pearls. She could not stop smiling.

Soon they were seated on a bench on a platform placed between the men and women's seating areas. A young girl approached them with a silver tray which held the engagement jewelry. Musa gave his (now fiancé) a gift of gold jewelry consisting of three rings, a bracelet and necklace. Musa received a silver ring to wear on his right hand during the engagement period. After the wedding he would change it to his left hand.

This is ceremonial since the families from both sides had already gone to the mosque for the contract which actually seals the engagement. The party is a public recognition of that agreement.

After they exchanged the jewelry, guests began to approach them giving congratulations. Soon Musa's brothers told us to go up and shake the couple's hands. As we went, the bride's father insisted we step up on the platform with them. We told him that would not be necessary, but he would not relent.

Trying his best to keep the spectacle at a minimum, John ever-so-carefully stepped up on stage in his *jalabaya* (which would be equal to wearing a long formal gown). I could not help but snicker. This was so wild. The whole village stood watching the foreigners crawl up on the platform and have their picture taken with the happy couple.

The father snapped the picture (which turned out blurry) and allowed us to immediately step down and rejoin the crowd.

Musa's friend who drove us told us to follow him and he would take us back home. As we were in the car, the driver stopped at the photography studio to confirm Musa's engagement photo session. It would take place at 2 a.m. Yes? Yes. We waited until Musa arrived and saw that everything was working out.

We found out later that Musa returned to the party after the photo shoot for a short time of dancing. Musa is quite shy so he put in the minimal time for dancing and ended the party.

As we were trying to wind down after the party, we reflected that we were the only foreigners–Christians, Americans, non-Nubians, nonrhythmics present among these beautiful people. How privileged we were to be there, to say a prayer for each one and to participate in their lives.

We visited with Musa the next day and noticed he had henna on both hands which marks him as a now-engaged man. It would be his job to secure an apartment and furnishings prior to the wedding. The wedding cannot take place until everything in the flat is purchased and completed which explains why engagements are typically 1 to 3 years in length.

Musa thanked us profusely for coming. We thanked him for including us. We told him that at the wedding, however, we were staying the whole time and both he and John would be dancing.

He smiled and said, "I don't think John will agree to this."

John laughed and said, "Musa, this is an important day. If you dance, I'll dance."

I, of course, will be videoing.

Culture Cue

Your other-culture friend may not be accustomed to direct answers. Many cultures are indirect and require a roundabout way of answering. Being aware of this difference may stave off future misunderstandings.

36

Zaheen · The Woman Who Prays
Plant Hope, Have Faith

I remember as a 7-year-old saying to my grandma, "Life isn't fair!"

She retorted, "Fair is where grown men in overalls throw cow chips for prizes."

That nugget of wisdom along with "If your nose itches, someone's comin' with a hole in his britches" have resonated in my mind over decades through various circumstances—be they troublesome or be they allergy.

There are days I cannot help but wonder, *How did I get here? In Egypt? In the Middle East? So far from family, friends, free refills?*

I was sitting with my new friends, the village ladies, drinking tea and doing my best to understand all of the percussive Arabic being directed toward me. A small boy about 2 years old came alongside me and gave me his biggest smile. I smiled back and watched as he tried to put his hand in my purse. He was looking for candy.

I had brought his family some sweets before and he had seen me take small packs of candy from my purse. He needed a refill. Before I could even react, one of his aunts smacked his hand and pushed him away as she gave him what I can only assume is their version of "what for" (another one of my grandma's phrases).

Things settled down and I chatted with them about their day. The oldest woman in the group, Zaheen, told her daughter, Mona, to go inside and get me something to drink.

I patted Zaheen's hand and told her not to go to any trouble. She shook her head no at me and began speaking in her Nubian tongue. I suspect she figured if I could not understand, then I could not decline. She was correct.

The other ladies were wrapping small pieces of paper into a cone that would be filled with roasted peanuts. The packets would then be put in a box and sold along the shore of the Nile to passersby. Microenterprise? Nice.

The 2-year-old began to make his way back to me, but he was given the eye by his aunt and he backed away. I smiled at him and told him I did not have any candy today. (No use getting in trouble for a well gone dry.)

Mona returned with a small tray and one single glass of tea in the middle. "*Itfaddalee!*" she said. (It is basically a phrase telling me to "go ahead.") I did. I noticed no one else got tea. When I asked, Zaheen said they had already had some earlier. They were perfectly content to watch

I just want to understand and to be understood.

me sip. We chatted about various things as I finished my tea.

The conversation waned. I began my exit conversation, which can take as long as the original visit so one must begin preparation at just the right time. I told them I had enjoyed our visit and the tea. They insisted I stay longer. We visited some more and then a second attempt was made with me standing halfway up. Before I could reach a full upright position, they motioned for me to sit back down.

"You go to bed too early anyway!" they said laughingly.

"When do you go to bed?" I ask.

"Oh, at 2 a.m. or so."

I told them I cannot stay up that late, but I get up earlier than they do.

One lady asked, "Why?"

She told me it is cooler at night and better to sleep in the day when it is so hot. Good point. I have, always been a bit of a night owl with no inclinations toward early birding. This could be my chance. These could be my people. Jimmy Fallon, them and me.

Someone asked me something else and I had to ask her to repeat it. I simply did not have some vocabulary yet so no matter how enunciated it was I could not understand. This is the part where I get a bit deflated. I just want to understand and to be understood. At times like this I have an out-of-body experience that sees the whole scenario:

A dusty village along the Nile. A small concrete and mud house on a dirt road. A group of women all dressed in black sitting on low stools in front of their home. Children running around playing with sticks. Then me. A very pale woman in khaki pants and multicolored, elbow/bum-covering shirt with sunglasses perched atop her blonde hair straining to somehow fit in, trying to make sense of it all.

Just how *did* I get here? I wll spare you the 99-cent Kindle version and just tell you this: raw obedience. Some days it simply does not seem fair to try to live this life out among people who are so different than we are, to be away from our daughters and family for extended periods of time, to somehow create a sense of normalcy in a place that boasts pharaohs and McDonald's simultaneously.

My attention returned to the group of ladies now staring at me. Apparently they had asked a question. The blank look on my face gave them their answer. They gave up and waved goodbye.

The next evening, I was walking in the village when the 2-year-old "candy" boy came running toward me. I thought he was going to ask for candy, but instead he pulled me to Zaheen's house.

As I entered the room my eyes had to adjust to the dimly lit space. Several women were inside sitting quietly. I looked for Mona and asked her what was wrong.

Through tears she said, "Mama is sick. Something's wrong with her head. She can't see and she's not making sense."

She led me into Zaheen's bedroom. Zaheen lay on her bed under a pile of fur-like blankets. The weather continued to reach

3 digits every day, but blankets were necessary when you were sick. I kissed her cheek and then sat on the end of the bed.

Her daughters were gathered together and began giving me the same report that Mona had. I gave each of them hugs and returned to the bed. We sat quietly as I again rested my hand on her leg and prayed for my friend in need.

Mona left the room and returned with news that the taxi had arrived. They would now take Zaheen to the hospital. I stood and moved out of the way as they lifted her up and helped her into the car. There was only room for two of the daughters to go. The others would come later.

As she drove away, I took Mona's hands and said, "I will ask God to help Zaheen." A tear rolled down her cheek and the moment left. The remaining sisters began to make arrangements to go to the hospital. I told them I would check in later.

The next morning, I went to see Mona to find out how her mother was doing. There in the chair as usual sat Zaheen. She smiled and motioned me over. She could see!

"Zaheen! You're here! Praise be to God!"

She grabbed me and hugged me fiercely. *"Al humdillalah! Al humdillalah!"* ("God be praised! God be praised!") She could talk.

Her daughters were sitting about her all smiling. I sat down next to them and told them how happy I was that Zaheen was with us. Mona looked at her sisters while pointing at me and said, "She is the woman who prays!"

They clucked in agreement. Zaheen thanked me repeatedly for praying.

I responded, "God is good." They agreed.

All arguments of "fairness" melted away. Why? Because just as a farmer may define what is and is not "fair" in life, he also has a deep sense of optimism. No one plants a seed without the hope that it will grow. No one tends and nurtures a tender shoot without the expectation that it will take root.

So I plant seeds of truth and understanding into dry, dusty dirt and water them (on some days) with my tears of self-declared unfairness, but not without hope…not without expectation.

An old Nubian Muslim grandma and a pasty Christian American mom became friends. That day we all declared God's goodness in our lives and hope grew.

Culture Cue

Do not assume because your other-culture friend nods her head and smiles that she understands everything you are saying. Try saying the same message a few different ways asking questions to confirm understanding.

Afterword

As I reflect over these pages, a lot of life has been lived within these stories. Missouri Pam would have been scared out of her wits to read her future life. Never once as she got on the plane did she imagine herself riding camels as an actual mode of transportation, laughing with a Bedouin *sheikh* as goat parts were pushed her way or fiercely loving people so very different (or were they?) from herself.

But a transformation has come. Through embarrassment, loss of comfort, laughter, pain of separation and at times bewilderment, God's grace has sustained me. The beautiful people in these locations have embraced me, taught me and cared for me. We've learned much from each other and shared deeply. God has been in the midst, my life is richer and I am grateful.

So what is next?

Hanshoof. (We'll see.) The world teems with amazing, creative, exuberant people. I choose not to live life from the lens of fear which creates skepticism and cynicism, but rather through the prism of joys yet to be discovered through sharing hope together in other-culture relationships. My journey serving and learning from these sincere souls continues.

I bought the plane ticket and journeyed to the edge of faith. I pray you, too, will step over the line embracing other-culture people wherever your adventure leads you.

May God's love and hope shine through us all.

Pam

Discussion Questions

Chapter 1

1. Have you ever lived in another culture? Describe the setting.
2. What emotions do you remember from the first few weeks?
3. If you have not, have you ever imagined living in another culture? Where?
4. What would compel you to live in a culture very different from your own?
5. What are some reasons people might give for not living in another culture?
6. List five character traits one might need to move to and live in another culture?

Chapter 2

1. Have you ever gotten lost in a new city trying to find a place? How did you feel?
2. Try to explain to the person sitting next to you how to get to a nearby grocery store without using any words, only gestures. Discuss after.
3. Do you enjoy shopping in new locations? What do you like to find?
4. Have you ever felt homesick? Where were you and what were the circumstances?
5. Do you know someone in your community from another culture? Do you think she is homesick? What are some concrete steps you could take to make her feel welcome?

Chapter 3

1. Moving to a new location, especially another culture, can be exciting and scary. Can you identify with what Pam was feeling in those moments?
2. What would you expect to have in your apartment in another culture? Do you think you could adapt if it were not like you expected? Why or why not?
3. If you could live anywhere in the world, where would you live? In what kind of home?
4. How would you describe yourself: open and trusting, independent and self-sufficient, slow to react and reticent, adventurous and carefree? How would each of these be a help and hindrance in a new culture?
5. What do you think other-culture people are feeling when they move into your community?

Chapter 4

1. Have you ever moved to a new place and had things go wrong? How long did it take to get things fixed?
2. Imagine being in another culture trying to get repairs done. What emotions do you think you would feel when trying to explain the problem, find a part or expect a certain level of craftsmanship?
3. What do you think of Kareema's hospitality and care for the Mortons?
4. Were you shocked when the workmen told John they would come "the day after Thursday," but they meant Saturday? Is there anything in your culture that other-culture people might misinterpret as well?
5. Does your other-culture friend know where to go to get something repaired? Have you asked?

Chapter 5

1. Do you speak more than one language? If so, name them.
2. Do you like learning another language? Why or why not?

3. Why would it be useful to speak the heart language of the people in another culture?
4. Have you ever met someone trying to learn English? What were your first impressions of him?
5. Is there something you can do to encourage your other-culture friend in her pursuit of learning your language?

Chapter 6

1. Name a traditional food that you eat on special holidays.
2. Why do you eat that particular food on that day? Is it a family tradition? Religious significance?
3. Can you list the groups of people in your town or city that have a different belief system than you do?
4. Do you enjoy learning about other cultures through food experiences? If so, why? If not, why?
5. Could you meet together over a meal and each person bring a traditional food? Explain why it is significant in your family and its religious significance (if it has any).

Chapter 7

1. Do you use taxis in your present location? Describe your experience.
2. Have you ever had an interesting conversation with a taxi driver? If so, share.
3. Why do you suppose Pam wanted to remain apolitical when speaking with Mohammad?
4. Put yourself in Pam's place. What emotions do you think you would have? How would you have responded?
5. Do you admire or resent someone who shares her faith? Why?

Chapter 8

1. Would you consider yourself someone who "lives to eat" or "eats to live"?
2. Who does most of the cooking in your home? Why?
3. If you have lived in another culture, did you learn to cook any of the local foods? If so, name a favorite.

4. Do you readily invite new friends into your home? Why or why not?

5. Would you be willing to invite other-culture neighbors into your home for a meal? Why or why not?

Chapter 9

1. Do you remember a teacher that you greatly admired? Who and why?

2. What do you think are three important characteristics of a good teacher?

3. What are three characteristics of a good student?

4. Are you adventurous when it comes to trying new foods? If so, name something "strange" that you have eaten.

5. If an other-culture host gave you something unusual to eat, what would you do?

Chapter 10

1. Have you ever had to take a job to make ends meet? How did you feel during that time?

2. How did Abdu's relationship with John benefit both of them?

3. Why do you think Abdu regarded John as a friend? Or Abdu as John's friend?

4. Do you feel you could be friends with someone with a different belief system than yours? Why or why not?

5. Is there an other-culture person in your life that you could share friendship with?

Chapter 11

1. Describe a social situation you were invited to, but were nervous about.

2. Pam describes her feelings before going to the farm, but how do you think the rest of the family felt? How would you feel?

3. What do you imagine dwellings are like for those who live in the Middle East? Did Aemed's satellite dish and Russell Crowe movie shock you?

4. How does the Aemed's hospitality compare to that of your culture, your home?

5. Would you describe yourself as a patient person who can go with the flow in unknown social settings or are you more of a "What's the plan?" kind of person? How would your answer affect the visit that Pam described?

Chapter 12

1. What is your favorite fast-food guilty pleasure?
2. Is there a place or a food you would miss if you lived in another culture? What is it?
3. Why do you think Rafita liked to spend time with Emileigh (17) and Aria (15)?
4. Is it worth making friendships in a location even if you know you will be there a short time? Why or why not?
5. Someone said there are "friends for a season" and "friends for a reason." Have you experienced this in your life? Are you willing to be a friend to an other-culture person for a reason or season?

Chapter 13

1. Have you ever moved to a new place without knowing anyone? How did you feel?
2. How did you go about making new friends?
3. Do you remember someone who showed you extra kindness when you were new to a job or location? Explain.
4. What could happen if someone new to a place does not make friends?
5. Is there someone in your neighborhood or community that is new? How can you be a friend to her?

Chapter 14

1. Do you like to do home repairs? If so, what specific ones?
2. Talk about your funniest or worst home repair you have experienced.
3. How do you normally react when things do not go according to plan?
4. How could your reaction help or hurt a situation in another culture?

5. Does your group have any home improvement skills that could be offered to other-culture newcomers?

Chapter 15

1. Pam describes her encounter with Miriam's situation as "crushing." What emotions did you have as you read this story?
2. Have you ever seen poverty up close? Explain.
3. What do you feel your responsibility is in helping those in poverty?
4. Imagine going home every day to this scene. How do you think you would cope? What emotions or reactions do you think you would have?
5. What are you grateful for today?

Chapter 16

1. Have you ever heard of henna before? Have you ever tried it?
2. What was your impression of this party? Is it an event you think you would enjoy attending? Why or why not?
3. Do you enjoy art from other cultures? What's your favorite?
4. Why do you think Pam agreed to the henna?
5. Are you open to your other-culture friend's traditions or experiences?

Chapter 17

1. How good are you at directions? Are you a "map person" or a "landmark person"?
2. Have you been in a social setting where you are unsure of the rules? What was it like trying to read social cues?
3. If you have children, do you give them opportunities to experience other cultures? How?
4. Would you say you are a patient person? How would being patient help other-culture situations?
5. Do you give your other-culture friend enough time to show hospitality and care as her culture would dictate?

Chapter 18

1. Do you like spicy food? What's your favorite?
2. What do you suppose the women in the English Club had in common?
3. In your opinion, what would make a group like this successful, meaning everyone felt valued?
4. What do you think it takes for a group of varied cultures to talk deeply with trust?
5. Discuss ways to build community and trust with other-culture friends.

Chapter 19

1. What is your favorite season? Why?
2. Did you know the five pillars of Islam before reading this book? Has that given you a better understanding of Muslims?
3. When you heard the phrase "Pakistani General," did any thoughts, emotions or images come to mind? What were they? Where do you suppose those ideas came from?
4. Was there anything in the story that surprised you?
5. Are you open to going to places that have people very different from you? Is that exciting or terrifying? Discuss.

Chapter 20

1. Do you enjoy looking for housing? Why or why not?
2. How do you think Pam and John felt trying to get the details of their contract worked out? How do you think you might have responded?
3. How do you respond in seemingly tense situations of negotiations? Do you remain calm, passionate, hostile?
4. Do you come from a passionate culture that argues one minute and loves the next? Describe.
5. Is there anything about your culture's housing system that might seem confusing to a new other-culture person?

Chapter 21

1. Have you ever traveled through a desert? Where? When?
2. What emotions do you imagine you would have if you were Pam heading out in the desert to a Bedouin *sheikh's* home?
3. What was your reaction when the *sheikh* said, "This is my wife, but if you are lucky you will be wife #2?" How do you think Pam's colleague felt? Did she respond appropriately? Why or why not?
4. If presented with a complete goat on a bed of rice, would you have eaten in order to accept this man's hospitality? What about the eyeball? Why or why not? What consequences could your actions have?
5. Do you want to live in another culture? Why or why not? If yes, what is keeping you from your dream?

Chapter 22

1. Have you been in a wreck? Briefly describe.
2. How do you think Pam felt as she sat in the cab of the truck surrounded by 50 Arabs all yelling and shouting? How would you feel?
3. Have you ever considered what it is like for others who live in another country to learn not only the language and culture, but also the laws?
4. Name the different ways The Advocate helped Pam through the ordeal.
5. Is there a way for you this week to advocate for your other-culture friend?

Chapter 23

1. Do you like road trips? Are you the "Let's just get there" person or "Stop and smell the roses" person?
2. When Pam's vehicle approached the village and the men were gathered at the entrance, what were your first initial thoughts?
3. When Pam prayed, "Lord, help us demonstrate Your love come what may" did that cause you to pause? If so, why?

4. How does your culture's hospitality compare to the hospitality shown to the Mortons? Discuss.

5. Discuss "the stick." How does fear affect learning? How does this affect a person's view of God?

Chapter 24

1. Have you ever used a squatty potty? Where?
2. Do you think it takes a special calling to go to difficult places? Why or why not?
3. Were you shocked that Abdelraheem asked John to "tell me the story?" Why or why not?
4. If an other-culture person asked you about your beliefs, would you be comfortable sharing them? Why or why not?
5. Is there a line you feel God is asking you to step across? Are you willing to act?

Chapter 25

1. Do you enjoy setting up a new place after a move? Why or why not?
2. What emotions do you think John and Pam had leaving Sudan so suddenly? How would you feel?
3. Have you ever had a sudden move or shift in your life that left you reeling? Explain.
4. How could you practically help a person who has been through such an experience?
5. Do you have an other-culture friend who has been suddenly uprooted or experienced loss? If yes, how could you help her?

Chapter 26

1. Do you have a nickname? Who gave it to you? Do you like it?
2. Salayla gave Pam the nickname "Tomato." How would you respond in this situation? Would you like such a nickname?
3. Is there anything in this story that stood out to you? Why? Discuss.
4. Why do you suppose Pam drank the hot tea?
5. Can you think of anything in your culture that might seem odd to your other-culture friend? Discuss.

Chapter 27

1. Take turns greeting each other in as many languages as members in your group can.
2. How do you think Pam felt when she could only understand portions of what Sadik was saying? How would you feel?
3. What did you think of Sadik's care for Pam since John was not with her?
4. Have you ever misinterpreted or misunderstood someone's story? Explain.
5. What is your other-culture friend's views on childbearing, family, etc.? Are they similar to yours?

Chapter 28

1. Do you prefer hot or cold climates?
2. Do you enjoy the climate you live in now? Why or why not?
3. What is the funniest home improvement story you have experienced? Share.
4. What do you imagine your emotions would be in a situation like this?
5. Do you have an other-culture friend who could teach you about plants from his country?

Chapter 29

1. What was your first car? Would you say you are a good driver? Would your friends?
2. What does it mean to "keep our circle wide"?
3. Name one endearing quality that Mokdee has.
4. Why do you suppose John continued to meet with Mokdee even though it could be difficult?
5. Do you know an other-culture friend who would like to learn to read your home country's language? How can you help her?

Chapter 30

1. Do you know the history of the town or city you are living in now? Share.

2. How do you think knowing the history of a place helps to better understand it currently?
3. Are you a person that has to have all the details before you make a move or can you operate with a level of nebulousness? Share.
4. How could your answer from #3 affect life decisions?
5. Has your other-culture friend expressed a desire to help his people in some way? How can you assist him?

Chapter 31

1. Does anyone in your group enjoy Egyptology? Ask him or her to share a fact or two about Egypt.
2. Why do you suppose the Nubians and "Dr. Jones" didn't get along?
3. Were you shocked at Ali's comments regarding terrorism? Why or why not?
4. Do you agree or disagree with Ali's rationale for a preschool? Explain.
5. Has your other-culture friend engaged in "difficult" topics with you? How did you respond?

Chapter 32

1. When do you like to visit your friends? During the day? Evening? Weekends?
2. Did you notice "It never rains here so why not make the balcony another bedroom"? Have you ever lived in a harsh climate? Where?
3. How would you have reacted to the ants in the sugar bowl?
4. What did you think of Pam's response to the "reading of the tea leaves"?
5. Do you know your other-culture friend's views on husbands, sons, men in general? If not, ask.

Chapter 33

1. Do you like attending weddings? Why or why not?
2. Are you a dancer? Would your friends agree?
3. How would you handle being stared at constantly? How do you think it would make you feel?

4. Why do you suppose Pam attended these weddings even though they could be awkward?
5. Would you go to your other-culture friend's special event even if it meant you were the only other-culture friend there? Why or why not?

Chapter 34

1. Do you have a Maxine in your life?
2. Do you think Farhat wanted Pam as a friend? Why or why not?
3. Have you ever met someone who was tough on the outside, but very tenderhearted on the inside? How did you discover this?
4. Why do you think certain people present themselves as "tough" and "gruff"?
5. Do you think your other-culture friend might be acting tough just to keep it together? Are you willing to love her and create a safe place of friendship?

Chapter 35

1. If you are married, how long were you engaged? How does it compare to the Nubian length of engagement?
2. Do you like the idea of the husband preparing the house and all its contents before getting married? Why or why not?
3. Do you like learning about other cultures? Why or why not?
4. Do you like experiencing other cultures? Why or why not?
5. Does your other-culture friend want to go to a party with you to experience something new?

Chapter 36

1. What are some folk sayings you grew up with? Share.
2. What do you think about Nubian social hours when they told Pam she goes to bed too early?
3. Have you ever wondered how you got where you are? What emotions did you feel? Explain.
4. Why do you suppose the women were moved that Pam prayed for Zaheen?
5. What are you hopeful for?

Acknowledgments

Special thanks to:

- *Kary Oberbrunner.* You are one ignited soul closer to your moonshot.
- *Jacob Rogers.* You love our daughter and others so well. You are an answered prayer.
- *Our extended family.* Your prayers, sacrifice and kindness allow us to live this life.
- *Ann Floyd.* Your editing makes me sound coherent and lucid. You are a gift.
- *Our colleagues.* You serve in hard and oft-forgotten places. It is a privilege to serve with you.
- *Our friends.* Your words of encouragement, prayers and shipments of chocolate chips have pulled me from the brink on more than one occasion.

Thanks for reading.

To book Pam to speak or order more copies of *One Plane Ticket From Normal*, go to: www.pamelajmorton.com.

Follow Pam:
Instagram @paminthesand
Twitter @paminthesand
Facebook Pamela J. Morton

Made in the USA
Middletown, DE
24 June 2017